Housing the Co-op

List of Contents

Housing the Co-op

A Micro-political Manifesto

Definitions

A—Co-operative
"A co-operative is an autonomous association of persons united voluntarily to meet their common economic, social, and cultural needs and aspirations through a jointly-owned and democratically-controlled enterprise." (1)

B—Co-operative values
"Co-operatives are based on the values of **self-help**, **self-responsibility**, **democracy**, **equality**, **equity**, and **solidarity**. In the tradition of their founders, co-operative members believe in the ethical values of honesty, openness, social responsibility and caring for others." (2)

C—Housing co-operative
"A housing co-operative is a co-operative society which corporately owns a housing estate in which each member occupies, or is a prospective occupier of, a dwelling." (3)

(1) International Co-operative Alliance (ICA), "Co-operative Identity, Values & Principles," accessed June 6, 2019, https://www.ica.coop/en/co-operatives/co-operative-identity.
(2) Ibid.
(3) John Hands, ***Housing Co-operatives*** (London: Castleton Publishers, 2015), 35.

Housing the Co-op is a micro-political manifesto for future livelihoods operated by and constructed through co-operative practice. It claims that housing production dominated by macro-economic interests and speculative markets must be countered by models based on co-ownership, co-production, and co-management of shared resources and capacities. By putting the focus on practices of co-operation and self-organization, the use value of local living environments is favored over the instrumentalization of housing as a commodity. Co-operative action thus offers viable possibilities to resolve the housing question in equitable ways and to reestablish housing as both a common good and a basic human right. Moreover, engaging with co-operative practice by means of housing production can also serve as a role model and active tool for promoting political and urban change from within the system.

In order to lay out the basic prerequisites for a broadened understanding of co-operative housing production, **Housing the Co-op** proposes three major claims that would enable more equitable housing developments and establish co-operative practice as a micro-political tool that could eventually impact macro-political frameworks as well. **A. Mobilizing Actors and Networks** claims that co-operative practice has to start with micro-political mobilization and building common networks. **B. Housing as Resource** states that equitable development can only be achieved if housing is generally recognized as a common good. **C. Reshaping Common Ground** calls for the transformation of private into co-operative property and for the formation of common ground as a social, ecological, and cultural asset. **Housing the Co-op** asserts that coordinated co-operative practice can ultimately effect broad systemic transformation by progressively inscribing micro-political action into macro-political frameworks and institutions.

Sidenotes Legend

→ •**G** = Link to Glossary
•**E** = Link to Essay
•**B** = Link to Bibliographic Reference

Housing
the
Co-op

Claims for
Action

Mobilizing Actors and Networks

Sidenotes

→ One of the most crucial co-operative principles, namely the democratic control of an organization following "one member one vote," can be traced back to century old traditions of managing common resources. While more obvious examples of such can be found along the various systems of commons ("Allmende") in the Swiss Alps, in her work the economist Elinor Ostrom shows that the management of collective resources through co-operative practices is a phenomenon that has developed all over the globe and in a variety of societies. Identifying "seven principles for managing the commons," she demonstrates that— apart from democratic control — co-operative practice relies on micro-political action that clearly defines specific agreements that guarantee an equitable and sustainable use of common resources.
•E—"We Are Cooperators: Building Social and Physical Environments through Co-operative and Collective Action," p.43
•G—7 principles for managing the commons, p.219
•B—Elinor Ostrom, *Governing the Commons: The Evolution of Institutions for Collective Action* (Cambridge: Cambridge University Press, 1990)

→ Unlike macro-political structures, which are based upon formal and institutionalized forms of governance, micro-politics operates on the level of the formation of attitudes, dispositions, skills, and capacities to shape behavior and produce subjectivities.
•G—micro-politics—p.217—production of subjectivity—p.219

→ In order to activate micro-political actors and networks, social role models must be redefined for truthful democratic representation to emerge. Specifically, gender roles form the primordial subjective structure of societies. Co-op practice questions this structure, showing new women role models for social leadership.
•E—"Donas da Terra: Woman Role Models in Social Leadership," p.199

→ Co-operative practice relies on micro-political mobilization, since it requires a sense for collective values and the active involvement of each member. Micro-political actors and networks form the very basis for self-governance and political action from below.
•E—"Freedom to Co-operate," p.183—"Shenzhen's Urban Villages," p.157—"The Mutirão Program," p.77—"Co-operative Development Goals," p.143—"Donas da Terra," p.199

A.1

Activate Micro-political Actors and Networks

Co-operative practice is built on the idea that participation forms the very basis for a democratization process from below. Negotiating between collective and singular interests, the formation of a co-operative therefore implies to build networks through active involvement of each member as a shareholder with one voice and one vote. Co-operative housing production thus relies on micro-political mobilization, as it claims that collective livelihoods should be co-produced and co-managed by each of the members of a group.

Mobilizing Actors and Networks

Sidenotes

→ Social capital evaluates the collective value of social networks while considering the contractual norms of reciprocity, including personal values such as trust, equality, willingness to cooperate, and transparency of shared information.
•G—social capital, p.220 — bonding and bridging, p.214— mutirão (mututal self-help), p.218

→ Social capital can be considered the most important asset for co-operative practice, as the formation of groups relies on strong ties between members (bonding) as well as on weak ties (bridging) with actors outside the group. While bonding guarantees the integrity of the group, bridging allows openness and permeability beyond the boundaries of the community.
•B—F. Guattari and S. Rolnik, *Molecular Revolution in Brazil* (Los Angeles: Semiotext(e), 2007)

→ Accessibility to co-operatives for various income groups and social milieus is key to the formation of an open and inclusive society. The case of the Mietshäuser Syndikat shows that co-operative organizations do not necessarily require start capital for becoming a member.
•E—"The Mietshäuser Syndikat: A Structural Answer to Anti-speculative and Self-Governed Housing Production," p.127

→ Co-operatives can be particularly effective in enabling social diversity and gender and racial equality, as co-ownership also entails empowerment and social security. The Mitchell Lama co-operative housing projects in New York prove that ethnic and social diversity can be better achieved through co-operative models than through policies for social housing.
•E—"Co-operatives within New York's Post–World War II Housing Crisis: Mitchell-Lama and the Promise of Equity over Equality," p.91

A.2

Bond and Bridge Social Capital

In order to establish co-operative practice in inclusive and equitable ways, ties between members have to be based on a regulatory framework that defines both common interests and personal responsibilities of each member, thus allowing the production of social capital. While a common contract bonds the group together, it should also be open enough to allow for bridging diverse interests and identities. Co-operative housing production is aiming at the creation of social capital, which assembles tangible as well as intangible resources for shared interests while simultaneously including demands of minority groups.

Mobilizing Actors and Networks

Sidenotes

→ The conditions of individual identity and collective belonging have become increasingly important in the context of capitalist production. While subjectivity functions as a "key merchandise" that is put together, developed, and manufactured according to market interests, it operates as the raw material for any and all production, as Felix Guattari argues. As commons are increasingly becoming enclosed and privatized, co-operative practice counteracts this tendency as long as it is based on transsubjectivity and the formation of a multitude.
•B—F. Guattari and S. Rolnik, *Molecular Revolution in Brazil* (Los Angeles: Semiotext(e), 2007)
•E—"Freedom to Co-operate," p.183

→ For the mediation between communality and subjectivity, sharing of resources and participation in the governance of commons plays a major role. To this end, co-operative practice involves direct social labor, which has been termed by Massimo de Angelis the practice of "commoning."
•B—M. de Angelis, "Plan C&D: Commons and Democracy," in *Collectivize! Essays on the Political Economy of Urban Form*, ed. M. Angélil and R. Hehl (Berlin: Ruby Press, 2013), p.126

→ In turning our attention to transindividual relations that constitute subjectivity, co-operative production makes possible politics with a new understanding of collectivity, not as an amorphous mass to be represented but as a multitude that acts and cannot be separated from its acting.
•B—P. Virno, *A Grammar of the Multitude* (Los Angeles: Semiotext(e), 2004), p.24

A.3

Mediate between Commonality and Subjectivity

While public and private interests are often played off against each other, an essential objective of co-operative practice is to establish arrangements between the private and the public realm, thus allowing the mediation between collective and singular interests. Consensus between diverse members is achieved through an ongoing process of negotiation that identifies the common denominator of various subjectivities. Particularly in capital-intensive sectors such as housing, the strength of co-operative practice lies in the fact that by sharing common interests and resources, the whole becomes greater than the sum of its parts.

Mobilizing Actors and Networks

Sidenotes

→ The main objective of capacity building is to produce human resources as well as organizational, institutional, and legal frameworks in order to foster effective self-development and autonomy.
•G—capacity building, p.214

→ UN-Habitat is the United Nations program for human settlements and sustainable urban development. Its main goal is to promote socially and environmentally sustainable living conditions for all. Since it is a massive challenge, capacity building becomes a crucial individual and institutional tool for achieving urban sustainable objectives.
•B—UN-Habitat – The United Nations Human Settlements Programme, http://www.unhabitat.org/knowledge/capacity-building

→ Even though capacity building is considered a priority by development agencies, its realization relies on sufficient funding and local networks. If we look at predicted future scenarios for urban growth, the strengthening of self-management and self-construction by local entities seems to be the only viable way to cope with the demand in housing and urban services.
•E—"Co-operative Development Goals: Urbanization Scenarios for Africa between Social and Technological Innovation," p.143

→ Capacity building is key to formulate micro-political needs and implement those needs macro-politically. The MCMV-Entity co-operative model in Brazil emerged out of a long-developed capacity-building process including horizontal (local) and vertical (legal) development strategies for the social housing sector.
•E—"The Case of MCMV-Entities in Brazil," p.99

→ Apart from the physical and technical capacity developed by co-operative practices to construct houses — particularly in Latin America — housing co-operatives rely and build on their members' capacity to self-organize. In the case of Uruguay's COVIVEMA 5, these skills have been supported by a strong labor movement and ultimately contributed to a widespread organizational network that has extrapolated the capacity to build solidly organized housing co-operatives.
•E—"COVIVEMA 5: A New Path for Co-operative Housing in Uruguay and Latin America," p.55

A.4

Enhance Capacity Building

Contrary to conventional corporations, self-governed co-operative practice is based on participatory, active involvement of each shareholder in decision-making and management processes. Through capacity building, each member can acquire and train various competences, such as administrative and technical knowledge or organizational skills. The integrity and operational strength of co-operatives relies on the capacity of each member to comprehend complex procedures and take on active roles in management processes. With their characteristic labor-intensive and complex management and maintenance setups, housing co-operatives can play a significant role in building capacity for the housing sector as a whole.

Mobilizing Actors and Networks

Sidenotes

→ The term *mutirão* originates from the indigenous Tupi language and stands for "joint effort," meaning the practice of mutual self-help work in order to obtain a result that cannot be achieved by one person alone. Currently, by extension of meaning, mutirão can designate any collective initiative for the execution of an unpaid service, as a joint effort. The self-help Mutirão model was embodied through the Mutirão co-operatives of the 1980s in Brazil and defines nowadays the inclusive process of urban initiatives of cooperation and solidarity.
•G—mutirão (mututal self-help), p.218
•E—"The Mutirão Program in Brazil: Co-operative Housing Production Intersecting Micro- and Macro-political Spheres," p. 77

→ On the most subjective level, co-operative practice activates social skills redefining deeply outdated social role models of genders, groups, and ethnicities. Co-operative housing strategies also fostered the empiric emancipation of gender structures in the Brazilian context.
•E—"Donas da Terra: Women Role Models in Social Leadership," p.199

→ The International Labour Organization states that skills for social inclusion are key for capacity-building agendas. The promotion of co-operative through co-operative enterprises and other forms of social and solidarity economy enterprises is emerging with viable and sustainable responses to the impact of climate change and the changing character of demographics, production, and employment.
•B—"Co-operatives," ILO, http://www.ilo.org/global/topics/co-operatives/

A.5

Develop Social Skills for Commoning Practice

Co-operative practice is a test bed for community building and democratic education. By giving emphasis to common interests and joint action, the social skills necessary to assume responsibility for collective concerns are developed. Co-operative and commoning practice thus extends the scope for the production of subjectivities and establishes new cartographies for life in common — with the realms of both social interaction and the built environment.

Housing as Resource

Sidenotes

→ One of the most important aspects of co-operative housing practices is the combination of collective ownership and nonprofit status, since it enables housing co-operatives to insulate their estates from speculative real estate markets. Through this, co-operatives contribute to a housing stock that is affordable for a very large part of society in the long run and basically transforms housing into a common resource. The case of Zurich shows that this is not a utopian vision – with the support of micro-political action and the resulting pressure on macro-political entities – can happen in one of the most expensive cities in the world.
•E—"Co-op City: Utopia and Pragmatism in Zurich's Co-operative Housing," p.167

→ Within the development context, housing is largely considered an asset for economic development. The definition of housing as a resource rather than a commodified good shifts the focus from the large-scale construction industries to the production of livelihoods by local enterprises and co-operative organizations.
•E—"Co-operative Development Goals: Urbanization Scenarios for Africa between Social and Technological Innovation," p.143

→ Housing is a basic human right as defined by the UN Charter, which is committed to uphold human rights of citizens by achieving "higher standards of living."
•B—UN Charta, http://www.unhabitat.org/the-right-to-adequate-housing-fact-sheet-no-21rev-1

→ The Sustainable Development Goals (SDGs) are a collection of seventeen global goals set by the United Nations General Assembly in 2015 to be achieved by the year 2030. Most of the goals can be achieved through co-operative practice
•G—Sustainable Development Goals, p.221

→ The New Urban Agenda is a document developed during the Habitat III conference in 2016 instructing the development, function, and sustainable design of cities. It upholds Sustainable Development Goal 11 – "Make cities and human settlements inclusive, safe, resilient and sustainable" – a claim that is incorporated in most of the co-operatives' agendas.
•G—New Urban Agenda, p.218

B.1

Claim Housing as Common Resource

Primarily defining housing as a profitable commodity is a fundamental trigger of global housing crises. If access to adequate and affordable housing is a right, it is time to reclaim housing from the logics of personal needs and make it work for collective interests. Instead of promoting speculative operations for a minority, the micro-political agency of co-operative practice can transform housing into a matter of mutual necessities and a resource for the common good.

Housing as Resource

Sidenotes

→ The story of the canton of Schwyz's over-900-year-old Oberallmeindkorporation shows that managing specific resources collectively and democratically not only benefits society as a whole but secures the interests of individual stakeholders as well. Co-operative practice appears to be particularly suited for long-term investments, where managing and sharing resources determines the well-being of multiple generations — be it for forestry or agricultural land in the case of Schwyz, or for housing production in the case of Zurich and Uruguay. Moreover, for these examples of co-operative housing production, the resources that are shared go beyond capital and materials: they also include valuable knowledge and expertise in co-operative organization.
•E—"We Are Cooperators: Building Social and Physical Environments through Co-operative and Collective Action," p.43
•E—"Co-op City: Utopia and Pragmatism in Zurich's Co-operative Housing," p.167
•E—"COVIVEMA 5: A New Path for Co-operative Housing in Uruguay and Latin America," p.55

→ Co-operatives are recognized by the International Labour Organization (ILO) as a means of implementation for the 2030 Agenda for Sustainable Development and the Sustainable Development Goals (SDGs). According to the ILO, ten of the seventeen SDGs can be achieved through the promotion of co-operatives.
•E—"Co-operative Development Goals:,Urbanization Scenarios for Africa between Social and Technological Innovation" p.143
•B—"Co-operatives," ILO, http://www.ilo.org/global/topics/co-operatives/

→ The shift from the science of "political economy" to the discipline of "political ecology" foregrounds negotiation processes between man-made and natural environments. In order to manage these processes in a democratic way, new forms of political organization and institution building have to be established.
•G—political ecology, p.219
•B—M. Angélil and R. Hehl, *Empower! Essays on the Political Economy of Urban Form* (Berlin: Ruby Press, 2014), p.12

→ Co-op housing production supports democratic processes that in return render mutual common resources for integrated communities. The Mutirão co-operatives are a best practice example for collective capital developed through democratic production.
•E—"The Mutirão Program in Brazil: Co-operative Housing Production Intersecting Micro- and Macro-political Spheres," p.77

B.2

Share Resources through Democratic Processes

The "delimitation" of material and immaterial resources has promoted an unequal distribution of power and wealth. Instead of securing access to knowledge, services, materials, and capital for a privileged few, co-operative practices allow for sharing and pooling resources in a more participatory and democratic manner. Sharing resources more widely and collectively will strengthen possibilities of micro-political action and break open access to vital elements of co-operative housing production.

Housing as Resource

Sidenotes

→ Rotating savings and credit associations (ROSCAs) — and its Ethiopian version called the Iqqub — show one of the many alternative possibilities of how capital can be generated and circulated by and for local needs. Co-operatively setting up a ROSCA by allowing every member to be part of the decision-making as well as running the operation on a nonprofit basis means that capital is seen not as an abstract asset but as a real item that enables investment and commerce within the local market. Furthermore, the relatively small size of capital investments needed from ROSCA members also offers an alternative to common schemes of microfinance without the common side effects of debt.
•E—"Co-operative Capital: Making Use of Collective Micro-fund Models for Housing Production," p.115

→ Co-operative housing schemes with collective ownership automatically produce a circular flow of capital. Due to the nonprofit status and the democratic structure of "one share one vote," potential surplus capital cannot be appropriated by an individual member or externalized as a financial product: it has to be eventually reinvested back into the co-operative and thus its local community.
•E—"Co-op City: Utopia and Pragmatism in Zurich's Co-operative Housing," p. 167

→ The organizational structure of the Mietshäuser Syndikat (Tenements Trust) is conceived as a merger of various groups in order to gather investment funds, which are invested according to the shared interests of the stakeholders.
•E—"The Mietshäuser Syndikat: A Structural Answer to Anti-speculative and Self-Governed Housing Production," p.127

→ Both in his seminal book *bolo'bolo* and his latest publication *Die andere Stadt* (The other city), Hans Widmer — who writes under the pseudonym P.M. — delivers models and ideas for environmentally and socially sustainable urban settlements based on co-operative practice and circular flows of resources.
•B—P.M., *bolo'bolo* (Zurich: Paranoia City, 1983); *Die andere Stadt* (Zurich: Paranoia City, 2017)

B.3

Promote Circular Flows of Capital Resources

The current mode of production has turned every monetary resource into a surplus-generating commodity for speculative markets that can be invested at a global scale and independent from its origins. Co-operative practice counters this trend by directing surplus capital back into the collectively owned co-operative and thus into local communities and territories. Such circular flows of financial resources not only spur local economies, they can also be a powerful tool against housing construction driven by speculation.

Housing as Resource

Sidenotes

→ In Uruguay, the co-operative housing movement has benefited extensively from the existing networks and organizational expertise provided by worker unions. Based on the idea of solidarity of labor, Uruguay's "Mutual Help" co-operatives have thus expanded the network of solidarity into the housing sector. Furthermore, the Uruguayan case also demonstrates that such a network can be shared — in solidarity — beyond national borders.
•E—"COVIVEMA 5: A New Path for Co-operative Housing in Uruguay and America," p.55

→ Solidarity networks can emerge through empowered social leaders who motivate and mobilize the masses for the formulation of common goals. The micro-political engagement of most women in the Brazilian context was able to integrate thousands of families and households, which in return generated empowerment of the community.
•E—"Donas da Terra: Women Role Models in Social Leadership," p.199

→ The International Co-operative Alliance (ICA) has been a main actor in supporting networks of solidarity both within and beyond national borders. The co-operative values and principles promoted by the ICA inherently reflect this attitude.
•B—"Co-operative Identity, Values & Principles," International Co-operative Alliance (ICA), https://www.ica.coop/en/co-operatives/co-operative-identity

→ Recent global economic and political instability has served to underline the shortcomings of the current development system and further confirm the necessity for an alternate or complementary development paradigm. The social and solidarity economy (SSE) is a viable solution to rebalancing economic, social, and environmental objectives.
•G—solidarity economy, p.221
•B— "Co-operatives," ILO, http://www.ilo.org/global/topics/co-operatives/

→ Co-operative organizations and other forms of models for shared economies, such as the Mietshäuser Syndikat, often establish solidarity funds for the redistribution of financial means for needy members.
•E—"The Mietshäuser Syndikat: A Structural Answer to Anti-speculative and Self-Governed Housing Production," p.127

B.4

Empower Solidarity Networks

Exclusive macro-level networks dominate many contemporary processes of economic and social aggregation. In order to make systems of knowledge and funding more accessible for co-operative housing, the power of networks has to be used to establish housing as a common resource based on the principle of solidarity. Making aware shared interests for all, solidarity networks — combined with co-operative practice — can empower micro-political action for both local and global initiatives for affordable housing production.

Housing as Resource

Sidenotes

→ Social-technical innovation was key to the Mutirão co-op housing practice in the Brazilian context. Developed by the Mutirão movement in the 1980s, social-technical assistance in Brazil currently supports the social-technical capacity building for innovative co-op housing solutions.
•E—"The Mutirão Program in Brazil: Co-operative Housing Production Intersecting Micro- and Macro-political Spheres," p.77

→ A new generation of housing co-operatives has become the driver for the latest phase of socio-technological innovations within Zurich's housing sector. Through civic engagement and bottom-up processes, these co-operatives are questioning the status quo of the common housing market and are experimenting with alternative forms of living together. The resulting innovations — both on organizational and architectural levels — have attracted worldwide attention.
•E—"Co-op City: Utopia and Pragmatism in Zurich's Co-operative Housing," p.167

→ The main difficulty for integrating technology into social practice is the lack of a narrative structure. For Bruno Latour, weaving together social and technological resources into an integrated whole constitutes the most important challenge for a sustainable future.
•B—B. Latour, "Technology Is Society Made Durable," in *A Sociology of Monsters: Essays on Power, Technology and Domination*, ed. John Law, Sociological Review Monograph, no. 38 (London: Routledge, 1991), pp.103–32

→ Urbanization in Africa and the social transformation that it engenders will rely on the means that can be deployed for capacity building and transfer of knowledge. As the current and future transformation of social and technological conditions is mainly driven by information and telecommunication technologies (ICT), the proliferation of self-organization and co-operative practice will depend on the formation of new institutional models connecting social actors with new technological means.
•E—"Co-operative Development Goals: Urbanization Scenarios for Africa between Social and Technological Innovation," p.143
•G—ICT revolution, p.217
•B—C. Perez, "A Green and Socially Equitable Direction for the ICT Paradigm," Globelics Working Paper Series 2014-01, p.20

B.5

Enable Socio-technological Innovation

Modern education and practice have, in many instances, detached innovation and the production of knowledge driven by practical skills and civic engagement. If this separation cannot respond to fundamental scarcities such as adequate and affordable housing, innovation has to be driven by micro-political action that is embedded in everyday life and necessities. Co-operative practice inherently captures socio-technological processes and thus unleashes the innovative potential of common housing needs and knowledge.

Reform Common Ground

Sidenotes

→ Probably contrary to general acceptance, collective ownership of land and other assets has not to be utopian or defined by political bias. As the case of the canton of Schwyz shows, co-operative ownership has not been driven by dogma, but by the pragmatic, common interest that certain assets — particularly things that are inherently linked to the limited resource of land — serve both the individual and the collective best and most equitably if owned and managed co-operatively.
•E—"We Are Cooperators: Building Social and Physical Environments through Co-operative and Collective Action," p.43

→ The case of the Mietshäuser Syndikat (Tenements Trust) shows that by owning and managing properties collectively the use value is favored over the surplus value, allowing to lower housing costs and foster equitable development.
•E—"The Mietshäuser Syndikat: A Structural Answer to Anti-speculative and Self-Governed Housing Production," p.127

→ Collective ownership offers a powerful alternative to the uneven distribution of land resources generated by private ownership. It allows citizens with small or almost no financial means to access territory that would normally be out of reach, as well as take part in decision processes that are normally executed by real estate developers. Indeed, a crucial part of the success stories of co-operative housing practices in Uruguay and Switzerland is based on respective models of collective ownership. Yet, as shown in both cases, this only works in the long run if the public sector plays a supportive role.
•E—"COVIVEMA 5: A New Path for Co-operative Housing in Uruguay and Latin America," p. 55
•E—"Co-op City: Utopia and Pragmatism in Zurich's Co-operative Housing," p.167

→ The architect Stavros Stavrides understands the term common space not only as a fundamental urban element that is open to, and governed by all, but as a place where social relations are reimagined and redefined in an equitable way. Expanding the idea and mechanisms of the commons to the urban realm, he calls for spaces that depart from classical models of private or public ownership and to move towards urban environments — such as housing and public spaces — that are co-operatively governed by and for the people that are inhabiting them.
•B—S. Stavrides, *Common Space: The City as Commons* (London: Zed Books, 2016)

C.1

Favor Co-operative over Private Ownership

The fundamental role that the current organization of territory and uneven allocation of land plays for social organization in general, and the production of livelihoods in particular, puts ownership at the center of the social question. To change the current condition of uneven distribution and foster equitable forms of development, privatization of property should be prevented and co-operative forms of ownership and land management should be favored. This is of utmost importance for affordable housing production, since the price of and access to land is one of the most defining aspects of successful co-operative housing production.

Reform Common Ground

Sidenotes

→ Including local citizens and the city administration, members of the COVIVEMA 5 housing co-operative in Uruguay took the responsibility to develop and improve the urban and social environment adjacent to their building. As a result, the co-operative has been able to implement a small park that is based on the needs, participation, and input of its surrounding community.
•E—"COVIVEMA 5: A New Path for Co-operative Housing in Uruguay and Latin America," p.55

→ The case of post-occupancy co-operatives in Ethiopia's capital, Addis Ababa, illustrates how, through co-operative practices, people take responsibility for their social and built environment beyond the boundaries of their private housing units to serve collective interests.
•E—"Co-operative Co-production: The Case of Post-occupancy Housing Co-operatives at Gotera Site in Addis Ababa, Ethiopia," p.67

→ It is not only ownership models that entail collective responsibility for common resources, communities, and neighborhoods. Access to the public requires individual and self-organized competence to manage pools of resources of collective use value that contradict the market logic of the city as private asset and commodity.
•B—R. Rolnik, *Urban Warfare: Housing under the Empire of Finance* (London: Verso, 2018), p.88
•G—social function of the city, p.220

C.2

Claim Responsibility through Collective Ownership

Apart from the various individual rights inscribed in land tenure titles, property ownership also entails social responsibility. Accordingly, the social or public function of private property pertains to collective ownership of co-operative organizations as well. Instead of just serving the needs of a closed group of members or a specific community, co-operative property has to be inscribed in the regulatory framework as a matter of public and collective interest.

Reform Common Ground

Sidenotes

→ Chinese urban villages are developed through self-organization on the basis of previously existing village structure. Even though these areas remain self-contained urban areas outside official planning frameworks, they nevertheless play a fundamental role in providing urban services and affordable housing units—a role, which is more and more recognized by governmental agencies.
•E—"Shenzhen's Urban Villages: A Micro-Political Tale from China's Mega-City," p.157

→ In combination with respective bottom- up processes, inscribing supportive measures for collective land use and ownership into planning policies is an essential feature of long-term success of co-operative housing practices. The successful examples from both Switzerland and Uruguay show how adequately implemented policies can incentivize and promote collective user rights and ownership. In Montevideo, for instance, the government issues long-term and low-interest loans to housing co-operatives. The city of Zurich, on the other hand, is following the guideline to give preemptive land-leasing rights on public land to nonprofit housing actors, which are, in this case mainly co-operatives.
•E—"COVIVEMA 5: A New Path for Co-operative Housing in Uruguay and Latin America," p.55
•E—"Co-op City: Utopia and Pragmatism in Zurich's Co-operative Housing," p.167

→ In order to maintain the social functions of the city intact, strategies ascribed to municipal plans can serve as a main tool of public control securing the implementation of adequate spaces of qualitative interaction, diversity, and inclusion.
•G—social function of the city, p.220

C.3

Incorporate Collective Land Use within Planning Frameworks

Counteracting the corrosive effects of speculative real estate markets on inclusive urban development, the allocation of land titles to housing co-operatives should be inscribed in official planning frameworks coordinated by local institutions. This would not only allow co-operatives to access central locations and gain visibility within official developments, it would simultaneously promote more inclusive, diverse, and mixed urban neighborhoods.

Reform Common Ground

Sidenotes

→ Many of Zurich's new generation of housing co-operatives have been pioneering new sustainable building techniques and more ecological ways of life, such as applying the "Minergie Standard" (a system of norms and certifications to ensure low energy consumption and a high share of renewable energy) from very early on, adopting the city's "2000 Watt Society" goals, developing housing layouts that collectively allow to reduce the square-meter-per-person ratio, or encouraging and enabling members towards a car-free lifestyle.
•E—"Co-op City: Utopia and Pragmatism in Zurich's Co-operative Housing," p.167

→ Co-operatively organizing the management of waste and collective green spaces, the example of Addis Ababa's Gotera neighborhood illustrates how the combination of co-operative practices and co-production can not only significantly increase a housing estate's use value but simultaneously contribute to a more sustainable and ecological management of resources.
•E—"Co-operative Co-production: The Case of Post-occupancy Housing Co-operatives at Gotera Site in Addis Ababa, Ethiopia," p.67

→ Elinor and Vincent Ostrom have coined and developed the idea of co-production since the late 1970s. Rather than separating service delivery in active producers (usually the public sector) and passive consumers (usually individual citizens), co-production argues for a synergy of responsibilities between public and private actors in order to make services and management of resources more use driven, embedded in society, and thus more sustainable in the long run.
•B—V. Ostrom and E. Ostrom, "Public Goods and Public Choices," in *Alternatives for Delivering Public Services: Toward Improved Performance*, ed. E. S. Savas (Boulder, CO: Westview Press, 1977; E. Ostrom, "Crossing the Great Divide: Co-Production, Synergy, and Development," *World Development* 24, no. 6 (1996): 1073–87

→ Housing co-ops are focused on the creation of long-term use value automatically contradicting the consumption strategy of surplus value followed by market mechanisms. The *Mutirão* co-ops created sustainable qualitative architecture with social identity and value despite economic scarcity, indicating the shift of economic paradigm to favor quality over quantity.
•E—"The Mutirão Program in Brazil: Co-operative Housing Production Intersecting Micro- and Macro-political Spheres," p.77

C.4

Take Responsibility for Sustainable Management and Ecological Concerns

By shifting the focus from surplus value to use value, property plays a significant role for long-term planning, particularly for sustainable development and the reduction of ecological footprints. Besides the needs of local communities, co-operative land and housing management can therefore take responsibility for ecological requirements on a global scale and initiate an alternative economic paradigm.

Reform Common Ground

Sidenotes

→ In the wake of the upcoming population increase in Africa, neither capital nor capacities are available to provide the estimated 700 billion housing units by top-down implementation. A shift towards self-organized housing practice would significantly contribute to democratic institution building as long as it is based on co-operative principles.
•E—"Co-operative Development Goals: Urbanization Scenarios for Africa between Social and Technological Innovation," p.143

→ The social asset of "belonging" is about not only social capital but also cultural and symbolic capital. Co-op practice enhances and strengthens the community for each of its members, which is indispensable for full collective functioning.
•E—"Donas da Terra: Women Role Models in Social Leadership," p.199

→ In Brazil the dichotomy between self-constructed informal settlements (favelas) and state-developed social housing exemplifies the urgent need for integrated housing politics that mediate between top-down organization and the local building culture established from the bottom up by the people.
•E—"Freedom to Co-operate: Urban Informality and Micro-political Counterrevolutions in Brazil," p.183

→ Richard Sennett offers a compelling narrative of why and how cooperation is a fundamental aspect of human societies. Most importantly, he sees cooperation not necessarily as a matter of moral or normative obligations but as a pragmatic skill and important societal ritual. From this perspective, cooperation is a highly inclusive practice, since it allows – although being rather complicated and challenging – discussing different views at eye level and ultimately negotiate ways how to achieve certain goals together.
•B—R. Sennett, *Together: The Rituals, Pleasures and Politics of Cooperation* (New Haven, CT: Yale University Press, 2013)

C.5

Establish Co-operative Properties as Social and Cultural Assets

While highly fractured and individualized environments are vulnerable to exploitative economic and political interests, they do not favor inclusive urbanization claimed by widespread micro-political support. Thus, for co-operative practices, the main goal for establishing common ground is the mobilization of local communities for participatory negotiations and democratic processes. The cultural value of these self-organized processes goes beyond the provision of adequate and affordable housing: co-operatively owned properties can serve as cultural assets and as a breeding ground for more inclusive, diversified, and equitable societies as a whole.

Housing the Co-op

Co-ops in Practice

We Are Cooperators: Building Social and Physical Environments through Co-operative and Collective Action

Sascha Delz

Imagine a world without cooperation to define goals, rules, and enforcement of our cultural and social lives: there would be hardly any educational system, no broadly accepted legal frameworks, and no systems of economic exchange. Imagine a world without collaborative efforts to produce commodities and environments that allow us to survive: we would still primarily eat berries, nuts, and an occasional rabbit, our clothing would primarily be made out of animal skins, and building complex urban environments including infrastructure and housing would hardly be an option. This might sound banal and simplified, but it addresses an essential yet often forgotten characteristic of how human civilizations emerged around the globe: cooperation is not only an intrinsic part of human nature and economic activities, but also has, over hundreds of thousands of years become a uniquely human expertise — an expertise that has contributed to how we interact to achieve common goals, how we develop social institutions, how we build civil societies, and how we compose economic systems and the production of goods. This general ability to cooperate has led to a variety of institutional forms of collaboration, such as, of course, co-operative practices, and by extension, co-operatives. So what is called co-operative practice, action, business, or organization in the following refers to the specific form of a social institution, namely the co-operative. In fact, humans have organized themselves into what we today could call co-operatives to produce services and goods according to their common needs for millennia. From this vantage point, the range of co-operative activities — from ancient co-operative practices to contemporary co-operatives — cannot be seen as fringe activities or as exceptions to the rule: they are, indeed, part of an essential story line of our species's development and ability to build civilizations through micro-political action and cooperation. One of these tales can be found in the Swiss Alps, where the Oberallmeindkorporation (OAK) and its institutional predecessors have been active in co-operatively managing local resources and producing goods for more than 900 years.

Cooperation Is an Everyday Practice with a Long Tradition

The documented story of the OAK begins in the year 1114 — more than 170 years before the foundation of modern Switzerland's predecessor, the Old Swiss Confederacy — when a letter issued by Emperor Henry V discussed a territorial dispute between the citizens of "Old Land Schwyz" and the Einsiedeln Abbey. The text mentions that the Old Land Schwyz's citizens, to stand against the powerful abbey, had organized themselves co-operatively to claim their land rights as a collective rather than as individuals. Located in the contemporary canton of Schwyz, today's OAK more or less represents what was then called the district of Old Land Schwyz.[1]

Yet, despite the remarkable discovery of the 1114 document, it is obvious that the activities described in the document were part of centuries-old co-operative practices to manage the community's collective properties and resources, namely the commons. A widespread phenomenon in the alpine areas of Switzerland, maintaining resources such as grazing land, forests, and water systems as commons often served rather pragmatic objectives. Faced with challenging topographical and climatic environments, alpine communities understood, for example, that taking care of the forests that protect the villages from avalanches in the winter makes more sense as a collective endeavor than allowing individual interests to destroy parts of these forests. Or, to avoid long-term depletion of precious grazing land that can only be used during the short alpine summers, farmers realized that a co-operative approach to negotiate and define — usually in great detail — the balance between individual farmers' interests, the number of cows, and the use of grazing rights enabled a beneficial production system for all stakeholders without losing the resource in the long run.

The OAK too is a result of such processes. Over centuries, the OAK's main activity has been the management and maintenance of a large amount of Schwyz alpine grazing lands and forests: today, within the overall 24,000 hectares under the jurisdiction of the OAK, over 8,000 hectares are used as grazing land, 9,000 hectares are covered by forest, and the remaining 7,000 hectares are nonarable stone fields and mountain areas.[2]

With regard to managing the commons, the OAK's activities are naturally reminiscent of the well-known case of the Swiss village Törbel as documented by anthropologist Robert Netting and further discussed by economist Elinor Ostrom.[3] While Netting's account describes in great detail how the Törbel community has been managing and organizing its commons over centuries — in this case, the first documents date back to 1224 — Ostrom is particularly interested in how a self-organized entity such as Törbel's community takes care of its commons, or more precisely, its common-pool resources (CPRs).[4] Described as "a natural or man-made resource system that is sufficiently large as to make it costly (but not impossible) to exclude potential beneficiaries from obtaining benefits from its use," a CPR is defined by two main elements: the resource system that has to be maintained (stocks) and resource units that are extracted by appropriators (flows).[5]

The main, rather challenging task of managing a CPR is to regulate access to, and extractions from, the commons without losing its productive capacities in the long run. Thus, the managing entities have to ensure the sustainable maintenance of the resource system, on the one hand, and protect the resource against exploitative and ultimately destructive unit extraction, on the other hand. To fulfill such management purposes, a CPR relies on a "provider" and a "producer." While the provider arranges the provision of the CPR as such, Ostrom uses "the term 'producer' to refer to anyone who actually contributes, repairs, or takes action that ensures the long-term sustenance of the resource system itself."[6] And indeed, "ensuring the long-term sustenance of the resource system itself" is a core feature of the OAK's self-determined commitments. According to its promoted agenda, the OAK is here to "preserve and maintain precious living environments," to "take care of our environment and resources," and to "secure the value of nature on our properties."[7] The maintenance and sustainable management of its resources is also part of the OAK's declared key purpose within its statutes: while it follows its members' interests to increase outputs, the OAK's main mandate is to "preserve its property in its substance" to secure resources for future generations.[8]

Apart from the rather traditional aspects of managing the grazing land and forests, the OAK has also reacted to present-day needs. Based on its core assets, it has started to diversify and adjust its activities over the past decades. The OAK has adapted its forestry practices to contemporary demands, such as the provision of CO_2 certificates. It has established an energy company that produces sustainable long-distance heating with wood coming from the OAK's forests. It has founded an agency promoting sustainable tourism in the region, integrating its gastronomy properties, its environmental assets, and its agricultural products into a local value chain. And since the mid-1980s, the OAK has also been actively involved in constructing and providing affordable housing throughout its land holdings.[9]

In this particular case, the mix of century-old co-operative traditions and contemporary production not only illustrates the ability of co-operative structures to conserve and innovate simultaneously, it also shows deeper links between micro-political organization, co-operative efforts, and building a civil society that go beyond particular historical epochs and political changes and affiliations. Indeed, through its long history rooted in managing the region's CPRs, the OAK's co-operative setup has not evolved from a particular political stance — which, in the case of the modern co-operative movement, is often placed in the spectrum of rather leftist, liberal politics (in fact, Schwyz is and has been largely dominated by conservative political forces). The history of the OAK shows that, from very early on, the members understood themselves as a co-operatively organized entity that secures pragmatic solutions for long-term stability — long before the modern co-operative movement came into existence. Thus, for the OAK, co-operative practice has not been an ideological choice, but the most adequate model to provide specific necessities and responsibilities towards its own members and the environment, as well as to accommodate general economic and social needs of the respective communities.

Last but not least, co-operative practice has also allowed a gradual but steady transformative process driven by a deeply rooted democratic culture. Profoundly embedded in the local community, the OAK has been a crucial part of the development of the whole canton of Schwyz. Its co-operative efforts and activities have been an intrinsic part of building and developing a civic society that is both politically independent (through democratic processes) and economically interdependent (through mutually beneficial arrangements). Beyond particular cases such as the OAK, stories like these indicate that cooperation is a fundamental characteristic of human interaction. As it turns out, contemporary research suggests that the way we cooperate, create social institutions, and build societies is a feature unique to the human species.

Cooperation Is a Fundamental Human Expertise

Cooperation comes so naturally to us that we often forget about how distinct it is, what has been achieved through it, and what would have been impossible without it. Yet, understanding Homo sapiens as a highly collaborative animal might empower an alternative narrative of human history that would counteract the habit of primarily writing histories of human achievement based on individual efforts, an array of decisions by singled-out individuals, or on a collection of asymmetrical assertions of power over others. Or to state it more bluntly: one of the main reasons why we have been so successful at building up complex organizations, societies, and civilizations is our particular, underlying ability to work together. Collective efforts are at the origin of almost every major cultural societal or economic paradigm shift of the last 15,000 years — be it the agricultural, scientific, industrial, or digital revolutions. While, of course, most species perform some kind of cooperation, the capacity to strategically work together towards a common goal — both beyond genealogical kinship and in large groups — is a feature essential to Homo sapiens.[10] Following developmental psychologist Michael Tomasello, humans distinguish themselves from other social animals in two specific fields. First, there "is what has been called cumulative cultural evolution. Human artifacts and behavioral practices often become more complex over time."[11] The second significant aspect of human development is the formation of social institutions, which "are sets of behavioral practices governed by various kinds of mutually recognized norms and rules."[12] These two characteristics are, in turn, strongly based on "a set of species-unique skills and motivations for cooperation."[13] According to Tomasello, the ability to cooperate appears to be "especially obvious in the case of social institutions," because they "represent co-operatively organized and agreed-upon ways of interacting, including rules of enforcement for noncooperators."[14]

Through these "agreed-upon ways of interacting," a great amount and variety of social institutions have found their way into human culture during the past millennia. And clearly, what we understand as co-operatives today are social institutions par excellence. While cooperation in general describes the human capacity to achieve goals together, the institutionalized form of co-operatives and their co-operative practices represent democratically controlled entities that are created in order to produce a specific service or commodity along agreed-upon rules. More precisely, a co-operative "is a voluntarily created organization of people, formed for the purpose of meeting their common needs through mutual action, democratic control and sharing of economic returns on the basis of individual participation."[15] But co-operatives are not only social institutions in the sense of reflecting and enabling general social human interaction towards a common economic objective. They also emphasize the ethical dimension of social behavior: in co-operatives, people usually work together for a common goal and the common good at the same time. The OAK's statutes, for example, dictate that while parts of generated revenues can be disbursed to its members, the resulting gains should also be invested into projects for the common good.[16]

As Jack Shaffer summarizes in *Historical Dictionary of the Co-operative Movement*, the co-operative mode of interacting and doing business has been, in various ways, based on practicing democratic decision-making, fostering human solidarity and mutualism, and building socially inclusive economies.[17] At a more institutionalized level, the most comprehensive stance on the inherent social and ethical values of co-operative organizations has been disseminated by the International Co-operative Alliance (ICA), which, as the largest federation of co-operatives worldwide, has promoted and advanced the co-operative movement since 1895: "Co-operatives are based on the values of self-help, self-responsibility, democracy, equality, equity, and solidarity. In the tradition of their founders, co-operative members believe in the ethical values of honesty, openness, social responsibility and caring for others."[18] And since co-operative organizations are not just aspirational or theoretical structures but primarily entities of real activity and production, the ICA has, over the last century, adopted seven principles for co-operative practice based on these values, namely "1. Voluntary and Open Membership; 2. Democratic Member Control; 3. Member Economic Participation; 4. Autonomy and Independence; 5. Education, Training and Information; 6. Cooperation among Co-operatives; and 7. Concern for Community."[19]

This ethical dimension of co-operative practice is an important aspect, because clearly cooperation itself is not a positive act per se. Humans also cooperate to do harm, to impose their group's interests, to exclude others from accessing specific resources, or to corrupt decision-making processes. So when sociologist Richard Sennett, for instance, states that "cooperation can be defined, drily, as an exchange in which the participants benefit from the encounter," and that these participants "cooperate to accomplish what they can't do alone," he is well aware of the challenges posed by the "destructive cooperation of the us-against-you sort."[20] This is why, in his book *Together: The Rituals, Pleasures and Politics of Cooperation*, Sennett proposes that the main way to counter such damaging forms of cooperation is to engage with the usually more demanding (and more beneficial) type of cooperation, which "tries to join people who have separate or conflicting interests, … who are unequal, or who simply do not understand one another."[21] In other words, rather than joining an "in-group" that collaborates to enforce and enhance opposition to a distinctly opposed "out-group," the spirit of a more inclusive way of cooperation is embodied by members of multiple social groups joining together to benefit the community in diverse ways. Doing so requires distinctive techniques and social skills that include "listening well, behaving tactfully, finding positions of agreement and managing disagreement, or avoiding frustration in a difficult discussion."[22]

Such socio-technological skills — as these techniques could be called — are clearly an expertise of co-operatives, since their members are trained to negotiate and discuss their interests democratically and on a regular basis. This constant exchange is part of the ethical dimension as well: co-operative members are — both implicitly and explicitly — confronted with all aspects of their co-operative activities and the related consequences within and beyond the co-operative. And while every co-operative establishes its own specific set of guidelines, rules, and ethical standards, there have been — as the ICA's co-operative principles show — some overarching values that can be attributed to various degrees to almost every co-operative. When looking at the OAK's activities and objectives over the past centuries, for instance, there is an apparent congruence with the ethical aspects described by the ICA's co-operative principles. This is, of course, no coincidence. Although repeatedly updated, the ICA's co-operative principles are based on iterations and experiences of hundreds of years of co-operative action. So while it is likely that most of the OAK's members are not familiar with the particular and actual co-operative principles as declared by the ICA, if one reiterates the principles — voluntary and open membership; democratic member control; member economic participation; autonomy and independence; education, training, and information; cooperation among co-operatives; and concern for community — it appears that, with minor adaptions, the OAK could directly integrate these principles into its own message and agenda.

Cooperation Is Society's Underlying Structure

Against the backdrop of ubiquitous collaborative human behavior, it is of course impossible to identify an exact starting point of co-operative actions and practices. What is clear, though, is that while the legal forms of what we understand as co-operatives today mainly started to gain traction in eighteenth- and nineteenth-century Europe, co-operative models of organization are as old as modern Homo sapiens. As Ed Mayo puts it in his effort to sketch "a short history of cooperation and mutuality," activities that could be described as co-operative practices according to today's standards have preceded many of the well-known examples started during the past two hundred years.[23] While it is important to acknowledge the impact and influence of historical landmarks — such as the foundation of the Rochdale Society of Equitable Pioneers in 1844, which is often referred to as the beginning of the modern co-operative movement — a "full history of co-operation and mutuality that weaves together the extraordinary ways in which the values of self-help and mutual aid have taken institutional forms across cultures" is still missing.[24]

In addition, since many co-operative practices outside of official legal frameworks persist today — either because not every nation-state's legal system officially enables, allows, or supports the co-operative model of organization, or because there is a substantial absence of public services and functions, which forces people to self-organize and operate outside of the legal systems out of necessity — it is of even greater relevance to understand our civilization's history by taking all forms of co-operative practices into account.

Describing and understanding the "ways in which the values of self-help and mutual aid have taken institutional forms across cultures," as Mayo suggests, could thus support a powerful, more organic and integral story of human civilizations based on mutual action, collective socioeconomic practices, and co-operative organization. Indeed, while the reasons that we know so much about historical co-operatives such as the OAK might be attributed to the particularity of Switzerland's history, as well as the Swiss affinity for filing and bureaucracy, there is no doubt that such histories of cooperation, collective action, and co-operative practices have been vital parts of past and present societies on all continents.

This means that apart from the habitual writings of history based on extraordinary individuals, achievements, and events, there is a somewhat ordinary — yet fascinating — underlying story that converges topics of general human behavior, evolutionary biology, economic practices, and societal development into an essential narrative of human interaction, cooperation, and co-operative organization. No longer perceived as the exception, collective action and co-operative practices would be understood as the indispensable connections that build and hold together everyday lives, societies, and entire civilizations.

1 OAK, "Chronik," https://oak-schwyz.ch/?page_id=244 (accessed June 4, 2019).
2 OAK, "Grundeigentum," https://oak-schwyz.ch/?page_id=955 (accessed June 4, 2019).
3 Robert Netting, **Balancing on an Alp: Ecological Change and Continuity in a Swiss Mountain Community** (Cambridge: Cambridge University Press, 1981); Elinor Ostrom, **Governing the Commons: The Evolution of Institutions for Collective Action** (Cambridge: Cambridge University Press, 1990).
4 Ostrom, **Governing the Commons**, 62.
5. See ibid., 30.
6 Ibid., 31.
7 OAK, "Alpen," https://oak-schwyz.ch/?page_id=189 (accessed June 4, 2019); OAK, "Wald," https://oak-schwyz.ch/?page_id=296 (accessed June 4, 2019); OAK, "Grundeigentum." Quotations translated by the author.
8 OAK, **Statuten Oberallmeindkorporation Schwyz** (Schwyz: OAK, 2014).
9 See OAK, **Ein Selbstportrait der OAK Oberallmeindkorporation Schwyz** (Schwyz: OAK, 2014).
10 Samuel Bowles and Herbert Gintis, **A Co-operative Species: Human Reciprocity and Its Evolution** (Princeton, NJ: Princeton University Press, 2011), 2.
11 Michael Tomasello, **Why We Cooperate** (Cambridge, MA: MIT Press, 2009), x–xi.
12 Ibid., x–xi.
13 Ibid., xiii.
14 Ibid., xiii.
15 Jack Shaffer, **Historical Dictionary of the Co-operative Movement** (Lanham, MD: Scarecrow Press, 1999), 39.
16 OAK, **Statuten Oberallmeindkorporation Schwyz**.
17 Shaffer, *Historical Dictionary*, 46–50.
18 International Co-operative Alliance (ICA), "Co-operative Identity, Values & Principles," https://www.ica.coop/en/co-operatives/co-operative-identity (accessed June 6, 2019).
19 Ibid.
20 Richard Sennett, **Together: The Rituals, Pleasures and Politics of Cooperation** (London: Allen Lane / Penguin Group, 2012), 5–6.
21 Ibid., 6.
22 Ibid., 6.
23 See Ed Mayo, **A Short History of Co-operation and Mutuality** (Manchester: Co-operatives UK, 2017), 5–7.
24 Ibid., 4.

COVIVEMA 5: A New Path for Co-operative Housing in Uruguay and Latin America

Michael Pfister

Uruguay has played a pioneering role for co-operative housing in Latin America and beyond. With the election of a progressive government in 2005, the co-operative housing movement has taken off at an unprecedented pace, almost quadrupling the amount of housing co-operatives between 2008 and 2017. The Uruguayan approach addresses two crucial aspects particular to contexts of emerging economies. First, faced with omnipresent housing shortages, top-down housing policies for rapid growth often create challenges regarding quality and equal distribution, making the resulting housing units less adequate and affordable for the originally targeted citizens. In contrast, by supporting co-operative practices, Uruguay's approach shows a successful story of scaling up a model controlled by bottom-up institutions that can address particular issues of adequate and affordable housing more directly and organically. Second, as in many other emerging environments dealing with economic hardship, self-construction of dwellings is mostly the rule and not the exception. In contrast to many governmental housing programs, the Uruguayan model of co-operative housing production explicitly allows self-help and auto-construction and supports it through an institutionalized support mechanism. Hence, as citizens design and build their own houses, they ensure that their homes correspond directly to both their needs and their financial capabilities regarding the cost of initial construction and long-term building maintenance. The Uruguayan legal framework not only unleashes the potentials of pooling resources in a collective way and of integrating co-operative members into planning and construction processes, it also provides real-life education and the capacity for building by laying paths that go beyond affordable and adequate housing units.

In 2018, I traveled to Montevideo, Uruguay's capital, to gain a better understanding of co-operative housing in Uruguay. Upon arriving, I encountered the topic even before I visited any co-operatives. It was carnival season, and I came upon a performance by one of Uruguay's typical carnival groups, the Murgas, clowns who use a traditional form of musical theater to satirize the most salient topics in politics and society. One song chapter was about the high cost of rent, leaving the Murga unable to afford a roof over their heads anymore. One clown suggested, "Let's form a housing co-operative!" Another one replied, "Forget it, for that we would have to work and even build the house ourselves!" and despairingly threw up his hands. The crowd roared with laughter. The concept of co-operative housing based on auto-construction had become mainstream in Uruguayan society. This particularly applies to the years since 2008, when the legal framework for co-operative housing was significantly improved and the construction of large amounts of new co-operatives began.

The basis for this development, however, was created as early as the 1960s, when the country was undergoing a profound economic crisis. Prices for Uruguay's agricultural exports were declining, and the subsequent removal of trade barriers favored the dismantling of formerly protected industries, resulting in rising unemployment and inflation. In addition, Uruguay's rural territory was, and still is, controlled by a small, long-established economic elite, a spatial-political structure that had long inhibited small-scale, decentralized rural development, leading to an increasing flow of migrants into cities.[1] Thus, over half of Uruguay's population lives in the capital, and the national urbanization rate is over 95 percent – the highest among Latin America and the Caribbean (LAC). In addition to these factors, Uruguayan leftist politics experienced dramatic uncertainty during the 1960s.[2] Neither of the poles of Cold War duality, communism or capitalism, were leading to constructive solutions: the ideal of a strong, centralized state became obsolete as Uruguay's comprehensive social welfare system, created in the early twentieth century, became unaffordable. Concurrently, conservative policies of austerity measures and the removal of trade barriers were producing disastrous results for the economy. Hence, due to a dwindling economy, accelerating rural–urban migration, and ideological disorientation within the political left, a quest for new concepts situated between entirely state- or market-based solutions was at the center of debates in the 1960s.

In response to these circumstances, housing activists created a form of co-operative housing based on assisted construction of housing by the co-operative's members themselves. The concept was based on the Rochdale Principles and values such as the concept of *ayni*, a practice of co-operative co-working of indigenous populations in Bolivia.[3] Furthermore, the movement has been strongly linked to Uruguayan worker unions, and crucially drew upon their organizational capacity.[4] The success of the first housing co-operatives in spite of the economic crisis helped the enactment of the 1968 housing law, which defined the basic characteristics of the Uruguayan regulatory framework still valid today. The state gives long-term and low-interest loans to housing co-operatives that can realize their project in two modalities. In the first, Ahorro Previo (Previous Earnings), which is aimed at middle-class citizens, members pool their savings to pay the required 15 percent equity of the loan and hire a private construction firm to execute their project. In the second modality, Ayuda Mutua (Mutual Help), aimed at lower-income, working-class citizens, members carry out the construction themselves, generating the 15 percent equity through manual labor. The Mutual Help modality in particular has a strong social interest, aiming at fostering community support, social cohesion, and solidarity. In both modalities, both the land and the building are owned by the co-operative, which in turn is collectively owned and maintained by its members in equal shares. While the system was highly successful in its first years, housing co-operatives came under significant pressure during the military dictatorship (1973–85) and only played a small role in the following years, during which conservative, neoliberal governments gained national power.[5] This changed with the election of the first progressive national government in 2005, which in 2008 introduced a significant modernization to national housing law, streamlining the process for co-operatives and allowing more government funding for loans. As a result, the number of housing co-operatives increased from 581 to 2,061 between 2008 and 2017. Almost 16,000 co-operative housing units have been built since 2005. By 2017, close to 3 percent of the capital's households belonged to housing co-operatives, as did around 1.3 percent of the country's total households, prompting the inclusion of a separate category for co-operative housing in the official national household survey in 2017.[6] Besides the government, co-operatives are also supported by two fundamentally important actors:

Institutes of Technical Assistance (IAT): In order to apply for a loan, co-operatives must have a valid contract with an IAT, which are private but officially approved interdisciplinary offices. They conduct technical and architectural planning and transmit knowledge about the organizational structure and decision-making of co-operative housing through regular assemblies. In the case of Mutual Help co-operatives, IATs provide crucial support in technical training. One of the best-known IATs is the Centro Cooperativista Uruguayo (CCU), which has been a pioneer of co-operative housing since the early 1960s.[7]

Federations: The national housing law encouraged the creation of federations of both types of housing co-operatives: FECOVI, the federation of Previous Savings co-operatives, and FUCVAM of Mutual Help co-operatives. Both provide general advice and political advocacy for housing co-operatives, as well as support in finding land. FUCVAM, however, is far more politically active and is engaged in a wide range of activities, such as a program promoting the international dissemination of the Uruguayan Mutual Help model to other countries in the LAC region and northern Africa, which won the World Habitat Award in 2012.[8]

A Real-World Example: Reviving the La Aguada Neighborhood in Montevideo

What is the reality of life in a contemporary Uruguayan housing co-operative? What are the main qualities and challenges for its members, and what are the biggest transformations within the movement as a whole? Many of these aspects are displayed in the co-operative COVIVEMA 5 (cooperativa de vivienda vecinos de Matriz Aguada), a Mutual Help housing co-operative of 55 housing units that was finished in 2017. The building is centrally located in La Aguada, the neighborhood surrounding Montevideo's harbor, an L-shaped structure, and the two halves are four and nine stories high. It has a clean and pragmatic appearance — the originally planned balconies were scrapped to save costs. Large warehouses are scattered across the neighborhood, many of which are abandoned, a testament to the country's deindustrialization. Yet the area is also marked by a significant residential housing stock of original, colonial-style buildings, many in states of visible decay. One of these huge old buildings, directly adjacent to COVIVEMA 5, is inhabited by low-income squatters, and in 2018 La Aguada made headlines for becoming a hub for Venezuelan refugees.[9]

Marcelo Irureta, Hugo Guedes, Leon Gonzales, and Martin Pignatta, who form the co-operative's current elected directive committee, are waiting for me in the building's open-air ground-floor access corridor that connects all entrances to the building. It is the unofficial main meeting point of the co-operative; many *cooperativistas* pass through or relax there, a mate calabash in hand. As Marcelo Irureta, the co-operative's current elected director, points out, the co-operative includes members of many diverse professions, socioeconomic backgrounds, and political beliefs. For instance, Irureta himself is an administrative employee in logistics, and other members include a university lecturer, factory workers, students, and an elected member of the municipality — a clear departure from the earliest housing co-operatives in the 1970s, in which all members often belonged to the same labor union and worked at the same factory. Nonetheless, members of COVIVEMA 5 are a tight community, bound together by the long and intense period of planning and construction.

The co-operative's central location, they tell me, is unusual for a Mutual Help co-operative and closely linked to the history of its formation. Informal planning began around 2005 by a group of neighbors in Montevideo who initially intended to organize themselves under the Previous Savings modality. After finding the piece of land in La Aguada and successfully applying for a government loan, the CCU collaborated with the co-operative to plan a complete architectural project. At a certain point, however, the group was unable to go forward with the project, as some of the members could no longer afford their share of the down payment for the loan, as the country's general economic situation was in crisis. Hence, the group converted their co-operative to the Mutual Help modality.

The architectural project already prepared by the CCU, however, corresponded to the hitherto prevailing logic of Previous Savings co-operatives: the central location and hence small lot size required a building height of up to nine stories to house the co-operative's demands. For Previous Savings co-operatives, this would not have been a problem, as construction would have been carried out by a hired construction firm. Mutual Help co-operatives, on the other hand, had traditionally tended to build one- or two-story houses, requiring less-sophisticated construction methods, as their members built their homes themselves. As such projects required more land, they were usually located on the periphery of the city, where large lots are available and affordable. Large neighborhoods composed of just such low-rise apartments became so common that the term *el dúplex*, the denomination of the typical co-operative two-story house, became a piece of identity for many pioneers of Uruguayan housing co-operatives.[10] A nine-story building constructed by a Mutual Help co-operative, however, had never been realized before, which created a good deal of uncertainty, as Hugo Guedes points out.

Yet the co-operative decided to go forward with the change in modality regardless of these obstacles. One motive was practicality: the elaboration of an entirely new project would have generated prohibitive new costs, and in addition building fewer stories would have mandated finding a new piece of land. The second motive was an increasing awareness by relevant actors such as FUCVAM and the CCU of the problems associated with low-density housing on the periphery, such as urban sprawl, socio-spatial segregation, and mounting costs for extending the city's network of infrastructure and services. For instance, these problems are on clear display with the co-operative Mesa 3, which can be reached with a one-hour public-transportation ride from the city center At the time of its construction in the early 1970s, many necessary amenities such as a school, cultural facilities, and shops were unavailable in the surrounding neighborhood, and the premises were not yet connected to infrastructure such as public transport or the sewage system.

Thus, these necessities needed to be extended by the city, and the missing amenities were included within the project, essentially creating a self-sustaining, encapsulated community. Furthermore, a few years ago, the entire premise was fenced in by the co-operative for security reasons, strengthening the impression of an insular community. In contrast, inner-city locations such as COVIVEMA 5's lot were already perfectly connected to services and there were high levels of vacancy — to some extent, due to a historic tendency in Montevideo and other LAC cities of investment being concentrated in separated, enclave-like areas of luxury and ubiquitous security measures.[11] Thus, there is an increasing willingness to "redensify" the inner city, and COVIVEMA 5 is a pioneer of this intent. Its inauguration was a prominent event, with participants such as the mayor of Montevideo, the president of the national housing agency, several officials of FUCVAM, and the national minister for housing, Salvador Schelotto. The latter said in his speech:

> From our ministry, we would like to express our deep satisfaction with this type of project in this type of location. Mutual help, altitude, density, high quality, quality of life for families and positive impacts on the neighborhood. This is absolutely exemplary and we will work towards having more housing co-operatives like this in Montevideo and the entire country.[12]

The Challenges of Construction

For the co-operative, converting to Mutual Help meant embarking on a project requiring very substantial contributions in time and work by all members. By law, each family or social unit must contribute 21 hours of work per week during construction. However, as co-operative members are directly involved in all decisions, additional time is needed for countless assemblies, administrative tasks, and assignments to support other co-operatives. Thus, this number frequently grew to around 35 hours per week for each social unit — besides the members' normal jobs — according to Marcelo

Irureta. Once the planning was completed, the construction process, which started in 2014 and lasted more than 37 months, was planned almost entirely by the co-operative.

A peculiarity of the Uruguayan system makes this coordination particularly demanding: The government loan is not given at once to the co-operative, it is rather given in pieces that correspond to specific construction modules. Money is only paid after the corresponding module has been completed and controlled on-site by a government official. For instance, the money spent on a staircase is only reimbursed after the structure is built according to regulations and confirmed by the government. Thus, co-operatives must consider the incoming funds for each part and plan the order of the process accordingly. Thereby, the co-operative's members participating in construction are continually educated by a construction company that conducts the most difficult tasks themselves in the beginning, but progressively leaves more tasks to the co-operative — a process that was successfully developed and refined over the years.

But in the case of COVIVEMA 5, the increased building height created new technical challenges. Mostly importantly, greater precision was demanded when laying bricks and pouring concrete, requiring significant effort by the co-operative, the involved construction firm, and — most importantly — by the IAT to professionalize these techniques. Furthermore, another consequence of the higher altitude is a higher construction cost per square meter, mostly stemming from a sturdier concrete structure and the cost of building elevators, the latter being necessary for elderly residents. These costs are currently not compensated by the government, but FUCVAM is demanding a respective change in the regulation: in their view, it is more affordable for the state to support these additional costs for higher altitudes in central locations than to extend services and infrastructure on the city periphery.

As is common in Mutual Help co-operatives, all members worked on all parts of the project, and the assignment of flats to members was made in a lottery only after the construction was completed, so nobody had an incentive to be more or less careful when working on certain apartments. A "loophole" with lower construction costs is that coverings of floors and walls don't need to be included in the initial project — therefore in each unit members applied individual floor tiles and colors on their interior walls after construction was completed, resulting in a diverse set of materials and colors within apartments. Marcelo Irureta, for instance, decided for black floor tiles and a combination of white plastering and exposed brickwork in his family's flat.

Each housing co-operative must include a multipurpose hall, which is primarily used to host the monthly mandatory co-operative assemblies. The assemblies, in which all members participate, serve as the principle decision-making mechanism: topics prepared by the directive committee or raised by members are voted on, and a protocol of each assembly must later be handed over to the ministry of housing. Through this mechanism, the government ensures that direct involvement of all members is actively exercised. At the end of my trip, I had the opportunity to attend such an assembly — the group of the directive committee invited me with the assurance that assemblies had become much quieter and more civilized since construction was completed. Yet the meeting was still loud and colorful, and the hall filled with a large crowd of co-operative members and their families. Among the topics discussed were the choice of floor tiles for the common corridors (which sparked the most heated discussion), the approval of one member who is soliciting a government subsidy for her monthly payment (which is agreed upon), and a theater group from the neighborhood who asked for permission to use the co-operative's assembly hall for rehearsals (which, after some discussion, was approved with the condition that members of the co-operative could see the show free of charge).

Linking Citizens with Urban Planning

At the end of my first tour of the building, we eventually arrived on the rooftop of the nine-story tower. The view overlooks the harbor bay of Montevideo and the old-town peninsula can be seen a few hundred meters away. Looking downwards, one can see the dusty courtyard of the L-shaped building, where construction for a planned public park started in 2019. The development of the park offers an insight into the role that housing co-operatives can play in linking citizens with urban planning issues. In 1990, the leftist coalition party Frente Amplio took power in the city government of Montevideo and has stayed in power ever since. In the following years, the city administration was reformed and decentralized: the city was subdivided into eight municipalities and eighteen neighborhoods with community centers to bring administrative services closer to citizens and offer them better participation. Besides numerous measures enabling citizen engagement, such as the election of citizens into local neighborhood councils, the city government is tendering two participative projects per municipality (*presupuesto participativo*) per year, each with a maximum cost of three million pesos, or close to 90,000 USD. Citizens can both make proposals and vote for two other proposals to be realized, one project in their own and one in another municipality. Thus, this concept, first introduced in Porto Alegre, Brazil, in the late 1980s, promotes direct citizen participation on a neighborhood level.[13]

For COVIVEMA 5, this offered the opportunity to summon resources for a public park in the courtyard of their L-shaped building, for which the co-operative elaborated a proposal. Three local architecture students and a professor designed the park, and neighbors could participate in the planning during various meetings organized by the co-operative. Subsequently, the project had to be promoted in the neighborhood in order to achieve enough votes. Christina Olivera, an inhabitant of COVIVEMA 5 and municipal councillor, describes this process:

> We did a lot of things like going from door to door to talk to the neighbors, going to the Sunday market, going to assemblies of neighboring housing co-operatives, going to schools and so on. In the end we achieved a very good result, 820 people voted for our project.[14]

Thus, the organizational capacity and effort by the co-operative COVIVEMA 5 as well as the collaboration with other housing co-operatives was crucial in facilitating the outcome. The assemblies were used to promote the opportunity of making a proposal, designing it, and partaking in the planning process, thus creating an important link between individual citizens and the city administration. The resulting project is a democratic compromise between various interests from the neighborhood: it will have a sports field, a corner for infants, and a rounded amphitheater-like stairwell. As Christina Oliveira says: "It's a public space — a space of living together [*convivencia*], of integration, where everybody is the same."

1 Tom Angotti, "Urban Latin America: Violence, Enclaves, and Struggles for Land," **Latin American Perspectives**, 40, no. 2 (2013), https://doi .org/10.1177/0094582X12466832.

2 Joshua Frens-String, "Revolution through Reform: Popular Assemblies, Housing Co-operatives, and Uruguay's New Left," **Historia y Problemas del Siglo XX**, no. 2 (2011): 27. Retrieved from http://www .geipar.udelar.edu .uy/wp-content/uploads/2012/07 /Frens-String.pdf

3 Gustavo González, **Una historia de FUCVAM** (Montevideo: Ediciones Trilce, 2013), 48.

4 Jennifer Duyne Barenstein and Michael Pfister, "The Professionalization of a Social Movement: Housing Co-operatives in Uruguay," **Built Environment** 45, no. 3 (2019): 382–97; Flávio Henrique Ghilardi, "El cooperativismo de vivienda en Uruguay y Brasil como parte integrante de la economía social," **XVI Congreso de Investigadores en Economía Social y Cooperativa** (2016).

5 Frens-String, "Revolution through Reform."

6 INE Uruguay, **Microdatos de la Encuesta Continua de Hogares 2017**, April 10, 2018, http://www .ine.gub.uy/c/document_library/get _file?uuid=72b74187-3cca-4c4f -9da8-c50ca77465c5&groupId =10181.

7 **Revista Dinámica,** no. 127, (October 2018); A. Moreno, personal communication, January 31, 2018.

8 González, **Una historia de FUCVAM**; "South–South Cooperation: International Transfer of the FUCVAM Model of Mutual Aid Housing Co-operatives," World Habitat Awards, accessed January 11, 2019, https://www .world-habitat.org/world-habitat -awards/winners -and-finalists /south-south-cooperation -international-transfer-of-the-fucvam -model-of-mutual-aid-housing -co-operatives/#award-content.

9 Guillermo Garat, "Un Caribe en la Aguada," **La Diaria**, February 3, 2018, https://findesemana.ladiaria .com.uy/articulo/2018/2/un-caribe -en-la-aguada/.

10 Lucia Anzalone "¿50 Viviendas Máximo?," **Revista Dinámica, no. 125** (February 2015); T. M. Leyba, "Entrevista a Miguel 'Tito' Leyba," **Revista Dinámica,** no. 125, (February 2015); interview with Patricia Petit, Arq. DINAVI. **Revista Dinámica**, no. 125, (February 2015): 28.

11 Angotti, "Urban Latin America"; John J. Betancur, "Gentrification in Latin America: Overview and Critical Analysis," **Urban Studies Research** (2014), https://doi .org/10.1155/2014/986961.

12 "Se inauguró Covivema: La primera cooperativa de ayuda mutua de 9 pisos," MVOTMA, October 3, 2017, https://www.mvotma.gub.uy /novedades/noticias/item/10009624 -se-inauguro-covivema-la-primera -cooperativa-de-ayuda-mutua-de -9-pisos.

13 See Presupuesto Participativo, http://presupuestoparticipativo .montevideo.gub.uy.

14 C. Oliveira, personal communication, February 25, 2018.

Co-operative Co-production: The Case of Post-occupancy Housing Co-operatives at Gotera Site in Addis Ababa, Ethiopia

Bisrat Woldeyessus

As cities and populations grow, the delivery of city services becomes more and more complex — and the role of co-operatives in mobilizing human resources and capital has become invaluable in certain places. In developing countries like Ethiopia, their contribution has multifaceted impacts on improving the quality and efficiency of "service deliver" in existing and newly built neighborhoods. In the case of Ethiopia's capital, Addis Ababa, new neighborhoods have been created at a tremendous pace and scale over the past fifteen years. A massive governmental social housing program was officially launched in 2004 and has since built tens of thousands of new housing units to address both the housing shortage and the overall low quality of existing dwellings. Built on individual ownership — the so-called condominium model — the program's housing block typologies have introduced a type of neighborhood that previously had not existed in Addis Ababa on such a massive scale. A newly built estate includes individual owners who, in many cases, have never met before moving in and who are responsible for collectively maintaining their buildings as well as the large amount of open space surrounding the housing blocks. Unsurprisingly, due to the breakneck speed of construction combined with a simultaneous lack of resources to deliver both crucial urban services and the chosen condominium model, many of the resulting neighborhoods have faced great challenges when it comes to maintaining and managing their public, collective, and green spaces. The Gotera Site, a neighborhood built during the early stages of the housing program, provides an example of a possible solution to these issues: co-operative practices and the collaboration of actively involved citizens and governmental agencies has led to significant improvements in the maintenance of collective neighborhood spaces. In a particular version of co-production, a post-occupancy housing co-operative (POHC) has entered several collaborations with the local administration to mutually provide traditionally municipal services. These arrangements have not only led to a significant improvement of the particular conditions but have also introduced an important platform of exchange, discussion, and collective action within the whole neighborhood.

Recognizing Post-Occupancy Challenges of a Housing Program

Confronted with an existing housing backlog of 233,000 units and a predicted further 223,000 housing units needed in the future, in 2001 the Ethiopian government started building up the biggest and most ambitious social housing program in the nation's history.[1] Working with the agency German Technical Cooperation (GTZ), the government initiated the Addis Ababa Grand Housing Program (AAGHP) in 2004, extending it to the Integrated Housing Development Program (IHDP) in 2006. Based on a comprehensive agenda, the IHDP intended to implement a program "that involves a combination of government financing and construction of housing in large and medium-sized cities targeted at middle and low-income households."[2] The program defined demanding objectives: it aimed to construct 150,000 to 200,000 housing units between 2004 and 2008, along with reducing so-called slum dwellings by 50 percent, generating 60,000 jobs, and fostering the formation of at least 2,000 micro and small enterprises (MSEs).[3] Due to its large scale and anticipated spatial and social impact, the program was also meant to "focus on conducive housing within conducive neighborhoods."[4] To achieve these goals, the program introduced the condominium model, which was based on a set of housing block and unit typologies, individual homeownership, and a corresponding mortgage system. To avoid any suspicion of unfair distribution of units, the administration decided to allocate the built units through a lottery.[5] Yet, as it turned out, nearly one third of the first-round condominium housing units built by the Addis Ababa city administration was not transferred to the lottery winners: a lack of financial means to pay for the mortgage, poor site locations in the outskirts, or a combination of both led many of the recipients to disavow their right to buy a condominium.[6]

Gotera Site, located on a former military camp in the heart of the city, however didn't take long to be occupied by owners and tenants. In this central area of the city, being awarded a unit through the lottery was considered a lucrative business: less than 10 percent of the initial winners are living in the units, while the remaining 90 percent of unit owners have decided to rent their apartments to more affluent citizens. Yet, as in many other of the newly built condominium sites throughout the city, the combination of individual homeownership, a high rate of renting out apartments, and a lack of public funding and management has resulted in a neglect of the usual supporting services that sustain a neighborhood beyond the housing units. Coordinated management of waste, parking, and green spaces, and the implementation of safety measures, have been basically abandoned at a municipal level since the construction of housing blocks finished. Yet, in a neighborhood the size of Gotera Site, with 2,150 families and 280 businesses in 78 housing blocks — each five stories high — the absence of services quickly exacerbates local problems. In the case of Gotera Site, it required a coordinated endeavor by the residents to address these challenges and take care of their collective needs. And so, in a remarkable effort, a group of residents has transformed Gotera Site from a rather disorganized and unsafe neighborhood into a better-coordinated, safer, cleaner, greener, and more walkable place to live and work through coproductive practices.

Addressing Service Delivery through Co-production

Considering the combination of citizens' actions and a governmental program to deliver a specific service, Gotera can be seen through the lens of co-production. As the theory of co-production suggests, the quality and efficiency of governmental service delivery improves when citizens are proactively involved. Elinor Ostrom, who coined the word in a workshop in the 1970s, argues that the synergy between government employees and service users leads to improved and more accessible delivery.[7] Gotera offers an exemplary case study to show the extent to which service delivery is improved through the involvement of citizens on the one hand, and the invaluable contribution of co-operatives in organizing individual efforts and promoting collective action on the other hand.

Based on the co-operative model, the Gotera Condominium Housing Unit Owners Association was launched by a few of the initial members in 2010, soon *after* Gotera Site's inauguration. After being formally recognized and registered by the Sub-city Co-operative Promotion Agency, it opened bank accounts, administered communal blocks, managed common spaces, and organized members. Since the co-operative actions only began after the members occupied their units — mainly to address remaining work to be done and collective needs — the co-operative practice applied at Gotera will be referred to as a post-occupancy housing co-operative (POHC). Because the POHC is responsible for delivering these services to the whole neighborhood, every household within Gotera Site is a member of the co-operative. This means that every unit owner has to pay monthly contributions but will receive, in return, general services — such as waste collection — that the public sector alone has been unable to effectively deliver. Thus, in a truly coproductive manner, the Gotera POHC's employees have been working with district officials as well as volunteers to provide missing services to the Gotera Site. Moreover, it has also introduced a number of general guidelines and practices regarding the use of common spaces. With this approach, the Gotera POHC has gradually improved the neighborhood over the past decade.

The Gotera POHC has collaborated with the Addis Ababa Traffic Office to redesign traffic signage, parking lots, and areas for restricted car use. Road signs have been mounted, and the POHC enforces the regulations by penalizing offenders. Another major achievement has been the management of waste. Often thrown out of windows, disposed of on the streets, or even worse, hardly collected, waste not only contributed to a seemingly disorganized neighborhood but also created unhygienic conditions. Together with district officials, the Gotera POHC introduced a waste collection program where each household can leave waste at its doorstep only two days per week. An additional co-operative, specifically established to take care of waste collection, brings the compiled household waste to a central collection point where the litter is sorted according to the available recycling categories. Residents cooperate by disposing of their waste according to the schedule but also by communicating to the Gotera POHC office when they see offenders. Similarly, the Gotera POHC has initiated the collaboration of the Community Policing Center with volunteers to monitor the neighborhood, and calls for meetings to create awareness when security concerns arise. By working with both formally recognized committee members from the neighborhood and other informants, the security and safety of the neighborhood has improved greatly. Finally, the Gotera POHC has clarified and structured the method of handling parking issues. Although the initial neighborhood design planned a provision of one parking space for every five units (excluding visitors), car ownership at Gotera Site has turned out to be on average one car per three units. This increased demand for parking has led to a rather uncoordinated appropriation of common spaces. Again, the Gotera POHC approached the district officials for technical support in identifying and redesigning the courtyards according to realistic parking needs. While these changes have dramatically increased the parking area, they have at the same time absorbed many of the original common green areas for each of the neighborhood's thirteen parcels. As compensation, a community park was developed on a roundabout that was initially designated for different land use by the city. As an additional effect, these measures have contributed to the fact that the common streets and walkways have now become more usable and accessible – a beneficial development for both social life and business activities.

The Gotera POHC's actions and its targeted engagement with the authorities have been highly successful. The Gotera Site was considered unsafe, chaotic, and difficult to manage. Common spaces were appropriated haphazardly for parking, dumping waste, storing items, washing clothes, sun-drying foodstuffs, and multiple social and cultural activities, resulting in congested common spaces and streets. Despite a slow start and rather fragmented member participation, the Gotera POHC has achieved what the public authorities alone were not able to accomplish: the estimated

10,000 people living in the neighborhood now have better access to infrastructure, services, and green spaces. Compared to adjacent neighborhoods, for example, all the streets are paved, accessible, and illuminated at night. Crime and theft have dropped significantly, parking disputes have become rare, and there is a designated public park within the neighborhood. Unsurprisingly, this has led to increased demand and the units' full occupancy.

Combining Co-production and Co-operative Practices

In rapidly urbanizing developing countries like Ethiopia, co-operative practices offer enormous potential for adequate and affordable housing. And as this example shows, the co-operative model does not necessarily have to be applied within the full range of traditional co-operative construction, co-operative ownership, and co-operative management. Even in cases of massively implemented governmental social housing projects based on individual homeownership — which is still a trend in many African countries — the active participation of POHCs can be considered a highly effective measure to improve the delivery of housing-related services that are often neglected by state actors after the construction of housing units. Looking at the Gotera Site, the coproductive actions initiated by the POHC have not only enhanced service delivery but also simultaneously improved the spatial and social conditions of the neighborhood as a whole. Based within the community, engaging with the community, and working for the community, the co-operative effort is able to address specific needs that a top-down administration alone might overlook or not even recognize. Furthermore, being run and owned by its members, the POHC has been able to find pragmatic solutions that break away from ideological approaches drafted in many planning and design offices (such as the ratio and distribution of green spaces and parking lots). Like many co-operatives, the Gotera POHC has faced challenges in successfully organizing and mobilizing members — after all, most citizens within the low-income brackets are busy making ends meet for their daily survival. Nevertheless, the obviously positive results have at least encouraged unit owners to comply with the guidelines and pay their contributions regularly. Thus, interestingly, participation has not necessarily occurred through the initial broad voluntarism of neighborhood members but by incremental steps that have implemented collectively accepted rules and regulations, by collaborations that have facilitated interaction between citizens and district officials, and by measures that have enabled improvements of the neighborhood on various levels.

The case of Gotera shows that POHCs, through a coproductive effort, can effectively and reasonably expand service delivery within a neighborhood. What is of particular interest in this regard is that co-production as a combination of co-operative practices and public-sector offices empowers a framework that goes beyond the mere technical implementation of certain services: while solely governmental or exclusively private actors would likely aim at serving their own particular needs — achieving set policy goals or generating profits, for example — a co-operative organization based in the neighborhood has different objectives. Directly driven by its members' and community's needs, a POHC is interested in providing necessary services and balancing social, spatial, and economic benefits at the same time. And because a co-operative's main objective is not to generate as much profit as possible for an exclusive group of individuals, it is clear that a coproductive setup that includes a co-operative organization on one side of the equation can be seen as a truly collective enterprise that links the "representational collective" in the form of government with the "collective representation" of citizens on the ground. In this respect, the story of Gotera Site strongly encourages the further investigation of the potentials of co-operative co-production — be it by enhancing the direct involvement of citizens in efforts of service delivery, by supporting policies that enable local administrations to engage flexibly and beyond strict top-down guidelines, or by promoting co-operative formation and capacity throughout the housing sector — not only for contexts such as Addis Ababa but for the production of adequate and affordable housing worldwide.

1 ORAAMP, **Structure Plan Housing Component, Improvement and Development Strategy: Guidelines, Regulations, Norms and Standards** (Addis Ababa: ORAAMP, 2001), 18, 23.
2 Federal Democratic Republic of Ethiopia (FDRE) and Ministry of Finance and Economic Development (MoFED), **Ethiopia: Building on Progress; A Plan for Accelerated and Sustained Development to End Poverty (PASDEP)**, vol. 1 main text (Addis Ababa: MoFED, 2006), 163.
3 German Technical Cooperation (GTZ), Ministry of Works and Urban Development (MWUD), et al., **Integrated Housing Development Program**, vol. 1, **Management Manual: How to Plan and Implement Integrated Housing Development Programs** (Addis Ababa: GTZ, 2006), 67–68.
4 Ibid., 54.
5 United Nations Human Settlements Programme (UN-Habitat), **Condominium Housing in Ethiopia: The Integrated Housing Development Program** (Nairobi: United Nations Human Settlements Programme, 2010), 26.
6 Ibid., 40.
7 See, for example, Vincent Ostrom and Elinor Ostrom, "Public Goods and Public Choices," in **Alternatives for Delivering Public Services: Toward Improved Performance**, ed. E. S. Savas ((Boulder, CO: Westview Press, 1977).

The Mutirão Program in Brazil: Co-operative Housing Production Intersecting Micro- and Macro-political Spheres

Patricia Ventura

In the 1980s, Brazil experienced a profound transformation of its political and social structures. The micro-political call for macro-political change motivated an entire generation to engage in the nation's re-democratization process. In this political context, and in regard to the housing question, the co-operative housing program Mutirão represents the most successful example of an urban macro-political transformation achieved by active micro-political mobilization. On the local scale, the consistent motions towards urban recovery, pursed equally by micro- and macro-political agents, had a powerful impact on the urban landscape as well as on the subjective inner landscapes of the involved inhabitants. As a result, the transformative experience of self-empowerment and capacity building was engendered. The social-spatial integration of disadvantaged, marginalized groups allowed their collective political voice to renegotiate the fundamental rights to housing and the city. The implementation of legal and constitutional frameworks resulting from the participative, experimental co-op approach prepared the ground for later social housing policy that was released two decades later, proving that micro-political organization can only reach its full potential if it also gains macro-political relevance. Thus the Mutirão projects can be considered a pioneering example for the micro-political territorial redefinition of integrated livelihoods, which, once empowered by local macro-political representation, holds the potential to enhance the macro-political policy-making process through its most democratic means.

The period from 1986 to 2002 in Brazil was marked by the political transition into a long-awaited democracy that demanded immediate engagement from the society as a whole. The end of the dictatorship came naturally with the rupture of all political schemes established by the military regime. After twenty years of oppression, public opinion now became indispensable, offering a lively platform for diversified discussion, engagement, and participation. A process of re-democratization of all institutions throughout the country took place. While society was experiencing the awakening of micro-political forces, on the macro-political level the country encountered the dissolution of administrative organs and valid policies, setting the stage for the rise of an authentic experiment in bottom-up public policy.[1]

The Mutirão co-op experience resulted from one such engaged civil movements and is one of greatest examples of the micro-political potential to engender macro-political transformation.[2] Apart from their relevant urban impacts, the Mutirão co-ops offer valuable insights about the political distribution of power and its consequence for our most intimate, subjective, physical, material, and human right to inhabit territories, allowing us to reflect upon the political as well as the personal responsibility for a systemic solution to the housing question.

From the Institutionalization of Popular Initiatives to the Mutirão Experiment in São Paulo

In regard to urban housing policy, one outstanding proposal among many others was the social housing production program Mutirão and Self-Management (Mutirão e Autogestão) introduced in São Paulo in 1989 during the governance of Mayor Luiza Erundina. Erundina was strongly supportive of social movements, and her political goals were based on a new agenda for urban inclusion through direct forms of civil engagement. Her political position and the stable financial conjuncture of São Paulo allowed her to implement ideas on a communal level using the city as an urban laboratory for social participation. Following the rule of three, her political goal was to interrelate good architecture, urban inclusion, and affordability. The scheme went far beyond single pilot projects, creating a vast arsenal of innovative prototypes depicting and materializing the vision of a democratic urban policy.

While social mass housing programs and public financing systems had failed for decades to offer sustainable solutions for the pressing housing deficit faced by Brazil's rapidly growing metropolises, self-engagement and cooperation formed by movements and NGOs developed into an alternative approach to tackle the massive challenges of urban inequality, informality, and segregation. The trajectory from micro-political expressions of desire to the institutionalization of collective urban proposals, however, was an unprecedented achievement and unique to Brazil's historical moment. How did the civil movements secure successful social participation in the constitutional process of the new republic?

In 1986, politically and socially progressive forces convoked the National Constituent Assembly (Assembléia Nacional Constituinte), whose members had been directly elected by the population to formulate Brazil's new democratic constitution. In addition, a mechanism of direct participation was introduced that allowed the discussion of constitutional amendments proposed by popular initiatives. By the end of the process in 1988, strongly mobilized social organizations representing millions of citizens influenced the final text of the constitution with 122 amendments implementing fundamental rights regarding education, health, environment, labor, human rights, gender politics, sexual diversity, and agrarian and urban reforms. The initial bottom-up public-policy process was only made possible by the equilibrium of forces of organized community interests and the public power in the process of reconfiguration.

In regard to urban policy, the unification of organized community forces was just as crucial as the communities themselves. In 1987, the National Movement for Urban Reform (Movimento Nacional pela Reforma Urbana) was established as a national platform consisting of innumerable housing associations that had hitherto been spread separately all over the country and fought independently for the constitutional right to housing and the city. The original manifesto of the *Reforma Urbana*, a paper formulated in the early 1960s and promptly suppressed by the military regime, was reintegrated into the political debate, fueling the urban movements with a strong sense of purpose and solid guidelines for change.[3] The so-called urban reform agenda became synonymous with an inclusive, regenerative approach for sustainable urban policy. Productive discussions were initiated through which urban fantasies could be collectively dreamed, while tangible proposals turned into constitutional amendments and experiments that would lay the groundwork for federal policies over the next decades.

The first implementations of co-operative housing initiatives were already taking place in the late 1970s, inspired by John Turner's arguments for participative models.[4] Financed by federal authoritarian military institutions (Banco Nacional de Habitação, BNH), programs for favela urbanisation (Profilurb) and embryonic tiny houses (Pro-Morar) as well as World Bank–financed projects (Site and Service) were tested but didn't allow for autonomy of self-organization, and therefore generated little impact. They did, however, attest to a slow shifting of the paradigm.[5] It was only during Erundina's mandate as mayor of São Paulo (1989–92) that new references of innovative social housing programs could be significantly implemented at a communal level. São Paulo's rapid growth resulted in the greatest housing deficit of the country, while the majority of communal representatives responsible for the urban sector strongly supported the cause of the National Movement for Urban Reform.

The municipality of São Paulo had, additionally, previously installed a communal secretary for social housing (Superintendencia de Habitacao Popular, HABI), which had access to specific funds – the Social Housing Funds for Irregular Settlements (Fundo de Atendimento a População Moradora em Habitação Subnormal, FUNAPS). A further measure was taken by raising taxes on commerce and services by 1 percent and earmarking the tax yields for urban development projects, equipping São Paulo's municipality with the necessary financial and professional resources to encourage original ideas.[6] With the best organized and mobilized housing associations and the best economic conjuncture and communal budget nationwide, São Paulo would become the predestined experimental ground for an unprecedented model of co-operative social housing interventions, among which the Mutirão program significantly stood out for highlighting the importance of self-management and solidary participation.

The Mutirão Modality and the Urban Impact of the Projects

The Mutirão projects were collectively organized as construction co-operatives. Citizens gathered together to build their own houses, neighborhoods, streets, basic sanitary installations, and city parks, as well as to urbanize informal settlements (favelas). The social movements were a melting pot of diversity since their actors came from all branches of society, forming a roundtable of academic professionals, politicians, financial agents, civil engineers, social workers, and citizens representing a mixed social strata of the population. For the first time, the community found professionalized, diverse support to confront exclusion.

Technical assistance agencies played the most significant role during this period. They were in charge of assisting and leading the community process while negotiating with the political institutions and authorities, thereby becoming the translator, the megaphone for the collective voice. As such, they helped create an entirely new collective language of co-operative manifestations, securing hereby the necessary communication between micro and macro diverging interests.[7] Experienced architects met a new generation of young architects and city planners, who served as technical assistants during the construction process. Technical assistance agencies helped organize the volunteers, whose builder groups were formed by a selective process begun by the associations close to the communities. Anyone with the will to engage could participate. The projects were designed collectively, according to the direct demands of the future inhabitants. Once signed up as volunteers, the families were fully integrated in the entire democratic decision-making process and development of the project as well as responsible for the management of transferred public funds. Here once again, the technical assistance agencies were responsible for the process of capacity building at every level of the complex building process. They assumed the role of interlocutor in the collective design process, disseminating technical knowledge in regard to construction techniques that could be implemented by volunteers, collectively managing funds and resources, and supporting social leaders to strengthen the community.

After three years of Erundina's governance, the first generation of the Mutirão program had implemented over 250 urban and social housing projects, assisting around 70,000 families and leaving a visible mark on the urban scale.

Such endeavors were only possible because the communal guidelines clearly favored the social function of the city over speculation on public ground. In consequence, the procedures attempting to conquer the city's central areas delivered most effective results. The selling of vacant public building for their original cheap historical price reduced site costs, while the expropriation of wastelands unoccupied for more than five years and the donation and subsidies of land allowed for projects to settle in the city center, reducing public expenditure for additional infrastructure projects and preventing peripheral settlements from developing. While the social mass housing programs of the military regime had resulted in the massive displacement of the city's poor, the city now assumed a confident counter-position of applied criticism, offering reliable alternatives to fix old failures.

The Mutirão projects further functioned as integrated neighborhood models of diversity. The insertion of not only a new project but an already mixed community of hundreds of families into existing neighborhoods called for complex negotiations on several levels. The surrounding environment accompanied the process, oftentimes over the course of years, opening up for social interaction and thereby surmounting segregative tendencies. Thus the buildup of the neighborhood community as a whole resulted from the dynamic process of exchange, collective mutual acceptance, and shared common ground, where poverty was no longer felt like a subjective synonym for criminality and the danger of the unknown. Consequentially, diversity was experienced as a strategy for security, significantly enhancing the urban quality of entire districts.

In addition to the increase of social value due to diversity, innovative prototypes of architecture and unique urban solutions were developed. Public social housing competitions were arranged for the first time, allowing for the presentation and discussion of new ideas. Unique urban layouts were implemented, for instance, through creative reconfiguration of generic ground plans. The bold use of innovative materials offered new approaches to the design process, allowing for flexible ground plans to accommodate the specific needs of the future inhabitants. The simplicity of the open spaces and green areas prioritized generating common spaces of quality, adding all the more to the significance of the interventions. The creative participatory approach offered stunning urban and architectural solutions, even under economically tight conditions, proving that simplicity and low cost do not compromise architectural quality, whereas the lack of freedom to experiment certainly does.

Although managing large-scale participation was a massive challenge, the first generation of the Mutirão programs attested to the outstanding potential of the co-operative approach as a method for possible sustainable urban recovery. The intersection on several scales within the city structure resulted in a healthy urban integration of the disadvantaged community, encouraging social mixing and diversity on the neighborhood level and offering architectural quality on the individual level. The projects were bold, confident, and singular, and so behaved their inhabitants. What's more, the co-operative approach eradicated individualist tendencies, for the individual was fully responsible for the collective creation of the built environment and the new sphere of the social. In consequence, a shifting of the perception of self within the larger society could empower the individual sharing that power, and thereby reveal the deeper social dimension and powerful impact of co-operative architecture.

The Radical Social Dimension of the Mutirão Program

Self-organization is key to effective co-operative strategies. The self-organization process of the Mutirão co-operatives did not start as a construction co-operative. For the Mutirão programs, the original goal consisted first in building a strong sense of community and defining collective goals beyond the simple need for shelter. The mobilization had to happen from the bottom up, as a movement of democratic faith in the right to inhabit and to exist in the "real city."[8] Prior to being an operating co-operative or even a political movement, the Mutirão community emerged as an existential movement that needed to gather political force to represent fundamental rights to housing that hadn't been fully constitutionalized or legally acknowledged. The political momentum was propitious, however, facilitating a favorable outcome for engagement.

In order to mobilize engagement, the social needed first to be re-invented, tested, and improved before any solutions became tangible. The path preceding the actual construction process was therefore crucial, but also unpredictable, fierce, and arduous. The lack of experience, resources, and clear guidelines demanded at the very least a clear vision of the necessary objectives. Social-technical assistance and community leaders assumed a crucial role in the motivation of human resources and creation of knowledge capital and capacity building to be re-invested in the collective whole. Since the basic sense of social belonging in the community was the only available resource, it was the most valuable raw material at their disposal. The Mutirão program was singular in the sense that it wasn't a program developed by the communal authorities but had been initiated through the bottom-up discourse of the movements that received support to further develop it. Its successful development, however, depended primarily on the prominence of a unified social formation and organization. The definition of guidelines and priorities defined the social configuration itself and therefore created a valid voice expressing authentic desires of future livelihood models, as well as manifesting them first socially and later materially.

The architectonic foundation stone of each project, for instance, was the construction of the community center, the "agora" for the entire future decision-making process. The design process and project management would take place here; the actual place of commoning marked the initial act. Complex multilayered co-op structures resulted from the Mutirão process. The creation of improvised, informal networks would later achieve a high level of co-operative professionalism. Co-operatives for fabrication and manufacture of construction materials, along with the construction co-operatives themselves, gave birth to a broader co-operative system that secured educational professionalization of sustainable craftsmanship, also reducing costs for future projects and enhancing the uniqueness of architectural expression. Some of these co-operatives survived, which enabled their integration into the formal economic system, creating autonomous jobs and professional perspective for young, engaged craftspeople. The social and knowledge feedback loops began during these first three years of the Mutirão program, influencing thousands of families and their future generations.

In light of the above, the Mutirão movements allowed the social dimension to be empirically reflected as the root principle for human development on multiple levels simultaneously. The program developed from a deeply psychological reorientation of the subjective self as part of a molecular structure to the self-organization of that structure as a new dynamic and permeable social formation up to the political institutionalization of the organized structure to express conscious desires and defend the fundamental right to existence. This alone allowed a deeper transformation of living conditions to manifest. As such, the Mutirão process represents the root definition and potential of micro-politics itself, which materialized here at its most fundamental level of applicability — in the attempt to find home, not simply shelter, and to re-code and re-territorialize the de-territorialized space of the common and of the self.[9]

Cooperation between Macro- and Micro-Political Scales

Based on the Mutirão experience, we can understand that micro-political organization can only unfold its full potential if it also gains macro-political relevance. In the initial phase of the Mutirão, we encountered an even equilibrium of macro- and micro-political forces, because in fact the macro-political authoritarian modalities of the military regime were dismantled so that an authentic democratic macro-political representation could mirror micro-political claims. In this phase, we can observe the attempt to acquire congruent up-and-down scales of corresponding micro- and macro-representation, functioning according to a social scientific Fibonacci sequence of the human endeavor to find, in this case, political balance. The social debates on the housing question and inclusive urban reforms were tested locally on the Mutirão models and led to significant constitutional changes decades later. While the first generation of the Mutirão model was successful in São Paulo and served as a reference for other cities, the implementation in less developed communities encountered great difficulties. The lack of federal financial and technical support for local governments clearly demonstrated the absence of legal frameworks and federal funding strategies necessary to establish effective urban policies applicable nationwide.[10] At that point, the social movements, activists, and politicians defending the urban reform agenda became fully aware of the great importance of drafting and implementing a legal master plan for urban regulations, which would pass ten years later, in 2001. Known as the City Statute, the constitutional right to housing and to the city was regulated and represented a milestone, enabling the executive power to define legal urban guidelines for the formulation of a new federal social housing policy. Its achievements culminated in the inclusion of the co-op model in the federal social housing program Minha Casa Minha Vida, which began in 2009.

But already during the 1990s, after Erundina's mayorship, although several hundred Mutirão projects could still be implemented,[11] even in São Paulo communal conservatism regained force, destabilizing the macro and micro uniform efforts for participative models, falling back on rather monofunctional and generic solutions for social housing projects and significantly curtailing subsidies for co-operative housing production strategies.[12] Nevertheless, the engaged professionalized communities, movements, and social-technical assistances were passionately committed to long-term prototypical projects that took on average five to eight years until full implementation. Yet one already perceives a clear tension between macro and micro forces, although the population, strongly moved by the solidarity gained from the molecular cohesion, firmly resisted, while the Workers' Party (PT) was still preparing its induction into the formal macro-political machine.

In fact, the growth of such tensions during the last two decades was revealed later: the 2016 coup d'état by former vice president Michel Temer and the macro-political consolidation of ultra-conservative forces since 2019 under Jair Bolsonaro's presidency are two particularly troubling examples. The shift of paradigms in social housing policies and the drastic disequilibrium of authoritarian forces further evinces the structural divergence of interests between macro- and micro-political pursuits. Instead of democratic representation of the basic rights and interests of the larger society, macro-political concerns now pursue the unfettered, ultra-neoliberal policy of the few. In other words, micro/macro dichotomy, whenever existent in the form of such polarizations of interests, is mostly of an economic nature. It is therefore insufficient to only strive for micro- and macro-political equilibrium without taking into consideration the dominant economic forces of neoliberal capitalism that manipulate both macro- as well as micro-political strategies to impede balanced, democratic power distribution. Here once again, the co-operative model exposes its unique resilience. Especially under unfavorable economic and macro-political conditions, co-ops mean organized resistance and collective self-representation, for they provide a robust foundation for micro-political efforts to grow institutionally, politically, and even economically.

But nevertheless, the co-operative approach requires self-awareness of this phenomenon in order to reactivate micro-political flows that can deliberately stimulate macro-political change. Both cooperation and micro-politics require a conscious interaction of the subject with the world, for the prevailing polarization concerns not only scales and configurations of power. It isn't merely spatial, nor is it political or economic. It is felt primarily psychologically, socially, and existentially in the distance between the disempowered, excluded self and the others. It requires therefore a priori the reintegration of the subject into the discourse in order to create permeability that results in engagement and self-empowerment. As we saw in the Mutirão example, the participative process expanded to become a transformative process on the core level of the subjective singular nature of the self. For it required the reorientation of the self, the expression of flexible subjective enunciations of empathy, and the reappropriation of humanistic codes, based upon which the reconstitution of the social could emerge and the conscious reassemblage of the common could take place, so that micro-political polyvocality could create macro-political vibrations.

In this regard, the Mutirão co-operatives established since the 1980s, hardly represent an alternative model for housing provision in the Brazilian context. However, the Mutirãos' specific modality, which requires complex reflections on the self in relation to sociopolitical, economic, and subjective factors of housing production, created a singular exchange that allowed its members to translate transpersonal desires into spatial implementations. What is achieved hereby isn't merely the participation of the community, but rather the active reconstitution of a powerful micro-political, social community that positions itself spatially, causing thereby macro-political resonance. In this sense, the Mutirão co-ops represent, in terms of quality, a valuable counter-model to dominant housing production strategies, for it rejects the mass production mechanisms of capitalism and dares to pronounce a singular yet collective answer to the housing question in the language of democracy.

1 N. G. Bonduki and A. P. Koury, **Os pioneiros da habitação social** (São Paulo: Editora Unesp; Edições Sesc., 2012).

2 The term *mutirão* originates from the indigenous Tupi language and stands for "joint effort," meaning the practice of mutual work in order to obtain a result that is impossible to achieve alone. E. A. Navarro, **Método moderno de Tupi antigo**, 3rd. ed. (São Paulo: Global, 2005), 422.

3 N. G. Bonduki, **A luta pela reforma urbana no Brasil: Do seminário de habitação e reforma urbana ao plano diretor de São Paulo** (São Paulo: Instituto Casa da Cidade, 2018).

4 J. Turner, "Architecture That Works," in "Housing by the People for the People," special issue, **Ekistics** 27 (1969).

5 A. Cardoso, S. Jaenisch, and T. Aragão, **22 anos de Política Habitacional no Brasil: Da euforia à crise** (Rio de Janeiro: Letra Capital, 2017).

6 Bonduki and Koury, **Os pioneiros da habitação social**; and N. G. Bonduki, **Origens da habitação social no Brasil: Arquitetura moderna, lei do inquilinato e difusão da casa própria** (São Paulo: Estação Liberdade, 1998).

7 P. Constante and I. Vilaça, **Usina: Entre o projeto e o canteiro** (São Paulo: Edições Aurora, 2015).

8 According to the urban reform agenda, the "real city" is a diverse, sustainable, and democratic environment that allows an inclusive society to flourish. The "real city" is one of the main claims of the National Movement for Urban Reform.

9 See the analysis of capitalism, here applied to the housing question, in G. Deleuze and F. Guattari, **Anti-Oedipus: Capitalism and Schizophrenia** (Minneapolis: University of Minnesota Press, 1983).
10 E. Maricato, **Para entender a crise urbana** (São Paulo: Editora Expressão Popular, 2015).
11 Between 1995 and 2003, 1.7 million social housing units were contracted and financed by several programs (PAR, Pro-Moradia, Apoio a produção, and Carta de Credito). Until 2009 around 14,000 housing units were built in Mutirão modality in São Paulo only.
12 M. Angélil and C. Siress, **Cingapura: Models in Circulation** (São Paulo: Schindler Global Award, 2017), 48–55.

Co-operatives within New York's Post–World War II Housing Crisis: Mitchell-Lama and the Promise of Equity over Equality

Kavita Kulkarni

> The decision to own is one of life's major decisions. It represents not only a desire to achieve housing peace but also an emotional experience. … It bespeaks freedom and security; it is tied up with pride, confidence, and the search for popularity or position. It connotes fun and gaiety, privacy without loneliness. It nourishes ambition and grants relief from the pressure of daily routines. It is the mysterious gadget that promises to resolve life's frustrations and conciliate one's desires.
>
> —Charles Abrams, *Forbidden Neighbors*

More than sixty years after New York City became the first municipality in the United States to pass fair housing legislation banning discrimination in both public and private housing, the city remains one of the most residentially segregated and unequally provisioned metropolitan areas in the country. The legislation, passed by the city council in 1958 and designed to disperse racial minorities into the private housing market, failed to integrate residents for very practical reasons, as complainants were simply unable to wait until a case had been settled to secure the housing they needed.[1] In this sense, anti-discrimination laws, although retaining symbolic value for a city determined to prove its commitment to racial equality, failed to provide actual material benefit for those communities most vulnerable to the post-World War II housing crisis.

Around the same time that the fair housing legislation was being passed, however, another piece of legislation aimed at resolving the housing crisis was gaining steam. The 1955 Limited Profit Housing Companies Act, also known as the Mitchell-Lama Housing Program, was primarily an affordable housing program targeting the moderate- to middle-income households that neither public nor private housing was serving at the time.

In one sense, New York City's postwar housing crisis was a matter of simple economics: the state of housing in many urban centers of the United States was characterized by greater demand than supply, a situation that was exacerbated in New York City by practices of urban renewal and slum clearance. But the value of secure housing—both in times of crisis and prosperity—extends beyond economics, as recognized by Charles Abrams in the epigraph to this essay: the feeling of homeownership grants peace and freedom, a sense of pride and relief. Indeed, these feelings were explicitly valorized in postwar homeownership propaganda circulated by the building industry, real estate boards, and "home" magazine publishers, all of which had a stake in emphasizing the emotional benefits of buying a home while minimizing the financial risks.[2] But even without these public relations efforts, it was undeniable that access to secure housing through homeownership not only conferred a sense of relief that one could not suddenly be evicted or have their rents raised or their home sold without their consent, but also gave residents the opportunity to determine to whom they would pass down their home in the future.

Access to these feelings of homeownership, however, was not a given; racism, affordability, and lack of housing stock were formidable barriers for many. The Mitchell-Lama Housing Program, enabled by legislation passed in 1955 on both the state and city levels in New York, was one government intervention that sought to lift those barriers. The program was intended to encourage, through public subsidies, private development of co-operative or rental housing for families whose earnings were too high for low-rent public housing but not high enough to afford housing on the private market. Eligible developers—whether commercial investors, co-operative associations, or nonprofit member corporations—were given assistance with site assembly, real estate tax exemptions, low-interest loan financing, and a modest but guaranteed return on investment (limited to 6 percent a year). In the case of co-operative housing, which makes up two-thirds of the city's Mitchell-Lama program, the developers would, after the building had become fully occupied and stabilized, turn ownership of the building over to the shareholders and their elected board of directors.

In addition to providing housing for a particular income group, the program also sought to reach secondary target groups, most of whom were deemed vulnerable to the housing crisis: families with children; families likely to migrate to the suburbs for lack of moderately priced housing in the city; households relocated by public or private action; ethnic minorities subject to discriminatory treatment in the private housing market; groups with special needs, such as the elderly and physically handicapped; and hospital and university staffs.[3] The achievement of these secondary targets, however, was tenuous, as the criteria for tenant selection for Mitchell-Lama programs was based wholly on income limits that were calculated on the basis of the annual rent: at the time of its founding, annual household income could be no more than six times the annual rent for households of three or less and seven times for households of four or more. Some artificial measures, such as architectural design—for example, in new projects, a higher provision of two- and three-bedroom apartments designed for families with children—were able to reorient the program accordingly, but otherwise buildings were filled according to general economic need.

For residents of postwar New York City who sought stable housing options but had been prevented from taking advantage of such opportunities by racial hostility and the lack of affordable developments and financing within city limits and in the suburbs, access to the ideal of homeownership through limited-equity co-operatives like the Mitchell-Lama program offered security that was hard to find otherwise. Residents of the Mitchell-Lama co-operatives built in the Clinton Hill neighborhood of Brooklyn in the early 1960s speak of the program as a stabilizing force in the area at a time when New York City as a whole was witnessing an unprecedented movement of white, middle-income households to the suburbs.[4] This stabilization, however, was in terms not of race, but rather economics: these Mitchell-Lama co-ops did not stop the trend of white flight from Clinton Hill in the 1960s, but their existence gave African Americans and Puerto Ricans of different class backgrounds the opportunity to attain permanent housing and to live in common alongside each other. One shareholder of the St. James Tower, a 326-unit Mitchell-Lama co-operative built in 1963, recalls how the projected racial split of his building—70 percent white to 30 percent nonwhite—ended up skewing in the reverse order within a few years of its construction as white families moved out, presumably after finding out how many nonwhite families would be sharing their space.[5] But racial integration was not the primary concern of the shareholders who remained—decent, affordable housing was. Another shareholder recalls her impression of the Mitchell-Lama co-operatives when they were built: "They were pretty decent. They were clean. People that lived in here were not wealthy, but they were hardworking. … It was definitely a step or two above the projects. That, everybody knew."[6]

Indeed, while public housing projects offered affordable housing for working-class people, they did not support upward mobility. The income limitations placed on public housing were such that the tenant was forced to vacate if their earnings exceeded a certain amount. Consequently, for the average resident with intentions of increasing their earnings over the course of their lifetime, public housing was imagined as a temporary shelter, not a place to establish a home. As noted in a 1963 article on the benefits of subsidized co-operative housing, forced departures from public housing projects added "another disruptive element to the urban living of many of the limited income families that [had] already been uprooted by renewal projects."[7] Of course, the reason for these income limitations was to ensure that over-income tenants did not occupy units needed by lower-income households.[8] This paradox of how to provide affordable housing for households with lower earnings while also providing the stability and security of a home as these households ascended economically was resolved by the Mitchell-Lama program, which ensured that residents would not be evicted once their earnings exceeded the income limitations. Instead, what was stipulated was the payment of a surcharge on top of monthly maintenance fees once a resident's earnings exceeded the cap.

Furthermore, because of the limited but guaranteed return on investment for developers, Mitchell-Lama projects were able to circumvent the risks associated with the open private market. With profit rates set at a 6 percent maximum, the irrelevance of opportunity costs meant that the racial composition of a project's tenants had no bearing on potential profit loss—that is, there was no need to be concerned with white flight or to make appeals to white morality in order to ensure the economic viability of the project. The only time race became a factor was with the very few large-scale Mitchell-Lama projects that galvanized pressure from the surrounding community or that were conceived as ideological experiments in racial integration in the first place.[9] The majority of the 123 Mitchell- Lama projects in New York City developed between 1955 and 1968, however, were of moderate size (400 units or less) and attracted a racial composition that either reflected the neighborhood in which they were located or contributed to a new racial demographic as white flight was taking place.[10]

By eliminating the obstacle of mortgage financing for developments in nonwhite neighborhoods, and by preventing lower incomes and racial bias from hindering opportunities for nonwhite homeseekers, the Mitchell-Lama program gave African Americans, Puerto Rican Americans, and other racialized populations in postwar New York City access to certain ideals of homeownership, offering stability, independence, and a sense of prolonged investment in their community. In the words of one shareholder addressing the ways in which the opportunity to own a home had value above and beyond its function as shelter: "If you had a stake in something, then you would probably … have more of an interest in taking care of it. You'd give it that extra little bit—as opposed to just renting an apartment."[11]

That these buildings were co-operatives also meant that residents were engaged in long-term collective work and decision-making—practices that generated a sense of autonomy and social cohesion within the building and the greater community. One shareholder recalls a moment of autonomous decision-making when he first moved into the co-operative:

> We had a fairly well-educated group of people. For instance, at our very first board meeting after the building was actually turned over to us, one of the shareholders, a Puerto Rican fellow, got up and said, "Well, the first thing we have to do

is get rid of all the incandescent lights in the public areas, because it costs a fortune. We have to change to fluorescent lights." Which we did, and over the years, that must have saved us millions of dollars.[12]

Having control over daily decisions regarding one's housing situation offered a feeling of self-determination that was hard to come by in public housing projects or rentals. And, of course, there was the social benefit of collective decision-making, which offered residents a sense of cohesion and relief from the experiences of alienation and marginalization that practices of racism and displacement begot. Notably, in a rapidly gentrifying neighborhood that witnessed the decline of approximately one-third of its black population in the first decade of the twenty-first century, the overwhelming majority of residents in these Mitchell-Lama complexes are to this day African American and Puerto Rican.[13]

Conclusion

In the last chapter of his book *Forbidden Neighbors*, urbanist Charles Abrams outlines a program for action in order to meet the postwar housing needs of racialized minorities. In it, Abrams addresses the protection by law of the opportunity to secure housing, noting that "one of the most difficult questions to resolve is when and whether to seek the outlaw of discrimination by statute."[14] Anti-discrimination laws and the rights-based discourse upon which they are founded certainly have made positive gains, especially in terms of signifying and making official the state's position of censuring the undemocratic treatment of minorities. But, as Abrams argued even back in 1955, these laws have all too often had little practical effect and have diverted attention away from interventions where real material gains could be achieved.[15] In the postwar era, many racial minorities living in New York City were faced with a paradox: they were gradually achieving gainful employment and middle-class status, but they did not yet have the equity to engage the urban private housing market and were being denied the financial subsidies and mortgage underwriting offered to their white counterparts by the federal government. And so, while investment in social engineering through anti-discrimination legislation served as the state's primary resolution to the barriers faced by racialized populations during the postwar housing crisis, what was needed more was government intervention on the local level to provide racial minorities with material opportunities to access the stability, security, freedom, and autonomy afforded by homeownership. The Mitchell-Lama co-operative housing program provided such an opportunity for New Yorkers of color without having to appeal to white morality, appeals which at their foundation not only centered and accommodated whiteness, but also created formidable hurdles for racial minorities to gain the autonomy to articulate their own experiences and desires.

1 Additionally, landlords and developers faced nominal punitive measures after being found at fault of discrimination and were able, moving forward, to find loopholes in their tenant selection process that would absolve them of any wrongdoing.

2 Sanders Kahn, "Rental Housing Threatened by Propaganda for Home Ownership," June 1952, Citizens Housing and Planning Council Archive, series 3.2, box 93, folder 2.

3 Barbara Woodfill, **New York City's Mitchell-Lama Program: Middle Income Housing?** (New York: Rand Corporation, 1971).

4 Brian W., in discussion with the author, December 2015; Brenda G., in discussion with the author, April 2016; Ivette F., in discussion with the author, April 2016. Names have been changed to protect the privacy of the individuals.

5 Brian W., in discussion with the author, December 2015; Brenda G., in discussion with the author, April 2016; Ivette F., in discussion with the author, April 2016.

6 Brenda G., in discussion with the author, April 2016.

7 Edward P. Scott, "The Co-operative Apartment in Government-Assisted Low-Middle Income Housing," **University of Pennsylvania Law Review** 111, no. 5 (1963): 657.

8 Ibid., 657.

9 For example, the case of the 5,881-unit co-operative Starrett City in eastern Brooklyn drew the concern of the mostly white surrounding community in Canarsie and East New York. Also, the 5,860-unit co-operative Rochdale Village in Queens was conceived by its sponsor, the United Housing Federation, as a utopian experiment in integrated co-operative housing.

10 Joseph S. DeSalvo, **An Economic Analysis of New York City's Mitchell-Lama Housing Program** (New York: Rand Corporation, 1971), 3.

11 Brenda G., in discussion with the author, April 2016.

12 Brian W., in discussion with the author, December 2015.

13 Tamy Cozier and Anniesofie Brochstedt, "Census 2010: A Dramatic Decline in Black Residents," **The Local: Fort Greene/Clinton Hill**, May 23, 2011.

14 C. Abrams, **Forbidden Neighbors: A Study on Prejudice in Housing** (New York: Harper, 1955), 353.

15 Ibid., 354.

Co-ops Within State Developed Housing Programs: The Case of MCMV-Entities in Brazil

Patricia Ventura

In 2009, Brazil introduced the social housing program Minha Casa Minha Vida (MCMV). It rapidly grew into the largest social housing program in the country's history. The program directed 5 percent of its budget for the development of social housing entities in an attempt to expand and integrate a self-managed model into the federal program. For that purpose the subprogram Minha Casa Minha Vida – Entidades (MCMV-E) was created, building on the tradition of the Mutirão co-ops of the 1980s and adopting the co-operative practice as housing production modality.[1] The implementation of a participative model within a state-developed social housing program symbolized a micro-political triumph accomplished by professionalized social and political capacity building acquired during decades of micro-political engagement. While this social intervention through macro-political mechanisms should ideally hold enormous potential for further democratization of urban policy claims, the reality of the massive MCMV program contradicts that very same purpose. The program promises access to housing but does not guarantee access to the city, preventing urban sustainability and diversification from unfolding. What led to these results and under which specific conditions could the co-operative approach play a significant role in mitigating these impacts?

It is impossible to understand the Minha Casa Minha Vida – Entidades model (MCMV-E) without first shedding light on the massive program MCMV itself. To delineate the program's key components and results, it is necessary to go back in time and revisit the initial claims for urban reform expressed by the civil movements and the Workers' Party (PT) in an attempt to establish democratic structures and urban social development since the 1980s in Brazil.[2] The inclusive social discourse led by PT, along with the civil movements organized since the 1980s, envisioned a federal sustainable urban policy, which amounted to one of the main election pledges of the party. When PT's candidate, Luis Inácio Lula da Silva, was elected president in 2003, the institutional and constitutional procedure to set in motion the massive shift in urban policies began, resulting in the launch of the program in 2009. However, an irreconcilable disparity arose between PT's initial objectives for the actual MCMV program and its implications. The program did indeed guarantee access to affordable housing, but it largely failed to promote social-spatial integration and urban regeneration. By tracing the historical line of policy development and political events since the 1980s until the emergence of the MCMV program, we come to understand the important role of the participative model MCMV-E, which was a last-minute addition to the overall program and is now one of the few resistance elements remaining of the spirit and objectives of the urban reform agenda.

From the Mutirão Experience to the Entity Co-op Model within the Federal MCMV Program

As a result of the civil engagement between the post-military period and the turn of the millennium, the political and economic implementation of a new national housing policy seemed achievable, and much effort was put into developing such a policy plan.[3] The Mutirão co-ops had offered the successful, empiric ground for essential claims about urban inclusivity, for capacity building and alternative housing models. Meanwhile, better-organized groups of social activists formed a civil institute called Instituto Cidadania (Citizenship Institute) during the 1990s. When Lula, the union leader and PT presidential candidate, joined the movement, it developed Projeto Moradia (Project Living) in 2000, which would become the guideline for the party's urban policy proposal based on the urban reform agenda. The achievements of the bottom-up policy-making process in the 1990s aimed for a major macro-political breakthrough on federal level. PT symbolically incorporated that hope, while Lula personified it.

The urban policy project soon became an integral part of Lula's presidential campaign. His ideas were supported by the participative approach of Projeto Moradia, which organized intense seminars, discussions, and workshops throughout the country. After three years, suggestions from diversified segments were gathered, resulting in a draft of the future government's housing policy plan.[4] The three main pillars of the policy consisted of: social and participative control, financial strategy for subsidies, and legal regulations to introduce urban instruments and control public land use to avoid speculative tendencies. During Fernando Henrique's presidency, the "City Statute" had been passed in 2001, ten years after its first amendment proposal legally constitutionalizing the right to housing and to the city. The creation of a ministry for the rapid implementation of legal urban guidelines and regulations would follow. The Ministério das Cidades (Ministry of Cities) was chosen to centralize all tasks concerning federal urban policies; President Lula inaugurated the ministry during his first day in office in 2003. Coordinated by PT frontmen committed to the urban reform agenda, concrete measures for implementation of an inclusive urban policy could be now undertaken.

Subdivided in four secretaries (Housing, Urban Planning, Infrastructure and Sanitation), the Ministry of Cities became the main institutional body in charge of urban regulation, representing a unique organ for that purpose in the country's history. Soon the Ministry of Cities organized the first conference of the cities, inviting over 2,500 delegates and about 3,000 municipalities to discuss and consolidate the overall objectives of the new government. At that occasion the board of the National Housing Council was elected, a participative platform for public discussions and proposals, the majority of whose representatives belonged to social housing movements. The first priority of The Ministry of Cities was to ensure the right to housing and to the city, upholding the City Statute. Pursuant to that aim, the ministry invested in qualifications for social-technical assistances and social leaders in small communities to help develop urban instruments that would be able to combat land speculation and facilitate access to land for social housing projects. The most efficient instrument became the development of differentiated municipal plans, which were elaborated by over 2,000 municipalities. Additional regulations weren't well defined yet – for instance, property rights impeded full practical employment of the municipal plans. Despite little visible impact, by 2005 the urban reform objectives had enjoyed considerable notice. From the federal level to local scales, productive solutions were slowly but uniformly implemented.

Regarding the financial structure for federal funding, in 2006 a major breakthrough was achieved. Popular initiatives begun in the 1980s proposed the creation of a National Social Housing System (SNHIS) equipped with no-return to low-return investment funds for subsidies (FNHIS) prioritizing low-income families. The bill was approved in 2005, finally mobilizing direct subsidy investments from Brazil's General Budget (OGU) which would serve to complement the low-return subsidy investments already provided by social security tax yields (FGTS). The Ministry of Cities was so far successfully committed to the urban reform agenda, and now the robust, colossal financial subsidy strategy FNHIS had just been endorsed.[5] However, between 2006 and 2008 the ministry would suffer a significant deformation of its initial policy project while public investments in the housing sector would triple, culminating in the launching of the MCMV program in January 2009. A look into the broader scope of political and economic events taking place outside the Ministry of Cities lets us evaluate their indirect impacts on the internal process of the agency.

One of the main reasons for the sudden policy shift was linked to the corruption scandal Mensalão, discovered in 2005. The scandal threatened the PT party with significant power losses in congress. Although Lula was reelected in 2006, the government had to cede several key positions within the Ministry of Cities to conservative members of the Progressistas Party (PP). By 2007, all secretaries of the Ministry of Cities, apart from only one — the National Secretary for Housing (SNH)[6] — came under the rule of conservative allies. After that, the commitment to innovative urban policies was fragmented, causing adverse disengagement from sustainable urban policy goals. The Ministry of Cities would aim instead for a policy of fast, visible, and pragmatic results.

Meanwhile, the macroeconomic development of the country was advancing at a rapid pace. The housing and construction sector formed a strong pillar of economic investment, contributing significantly to that progress. Lula's overall political strategy, on the other hand, was centered on national development projects aiming to eradicate extreme poverty and mitigate social inequality by installing a basic welfare-state system and by accelerating economic growth.[7] His approach was based on left-right coalitions, negotiations with stakeholders, and moderate financial reforms respecting market institutions in order to guarantee macroeconomic stability so that excluded sections of society could be integrated into the formal labor market.

Against this background, the program MCMV was drafted during the eventful year of 2008, while the US subprime mortgage financial crisis became global, threatening to impact the Brazilian economy, specifically the construction and housing sector. Designed by the Ministry of Finance to support the private housing market and prevent Brazil from falling victim to global economic fluctuations, a light version of the program was presented to the Ministry of Cities. The emergency-investment support program for the housing sector was immediately endorsed by the Ministry of Cities, upscaled by Lula, and redefined as a social housing policy project with focus on the low-income segment, resulting in 2009 in the launch of the program Minha Casa Minha Vida — MCMV, as we know it today.[8] The program's concept allows middle- to low-income families to access the housing credit market, while up to 100 percent of subsidies for the lowest income class would be financed by the large FNHIS funds, thereby closing the circuit of consumption for all strata of society. With high subsidy capital, private contractors are commissioned to produce mass housing for the low-income population. Economic growth is stimulated and quick access to affordable housing thereby guaranteed. Considering all factors, the persuasive lobby work of big private construction companies,[9] the goal of macroeconomic stability, the high housing deficit of the country — which was surveyed for the first time[10] — and the available large public investment capacity for social housing, the MCMV program proposal would emerge as a deus ex machina answer to the intricate housing question, merely solved by a macro-political and macroeconomic arrangement.

As soon as the organized social housing movements and the National Forum for Urban Reform realized that they were excluded from the development of the massive social housing program, their fierce mobilization and protests resulted in renewed negotiations. They argued for the integration of a participative, self-organized model and required the urban reform agenda to be included in the qualitative regulations of the program since it had proven to be a solid guideline for steady and sustainable improvement. However, the MCMV regulations were developed at such an accelerated pace that only immature qualitative norms found consideration, while quantitative factors were minutely defined. Accordingly, the varying demands of different movements were given equal consideration solely in terms of figures, resulting in 5 percent of the entire program budget being granted as direct subsidies for self-organized entities functioning in a similar manner to the Mutirão model. Although not nearly enough to guarantee the quality requirements proposed by the urban reform agenda, the subprogram MCMV-E was eventually integrated into the commercial social housing program due to the relentless militancy of the social movements, and thereby represented in itself only a symbolic mark of engagement in pursuit of sustainable urban reform.

In short, the formulation of the MCMV program was the result of an economic-political alliance that attempted to quickly solve the country's housing deficit, while not only stabilizing the economy but also launching a counter-cyclic development package to retaliate against the global crisis. A massive program was mounted, while sustainable urban policy considerations were fully excluded from the proposal. However, it was due to long years of patient and diligent institutional implementation of urban policy instruments, initially created for the purpose of innovative urban regeneration, that the MCMV program could be employed at such a high level of efficiency. Paradoxically, the subprogram MCMV-E, which was solely committed to sustainable urban solutions, did not achieve such a high level of applicability within the functioning mechanisms of MCMV. A closer look into the operational setups reveals the reasons for such contradictions.

MCMV-E Bridging Multiple Institutional Actors and Inflexible Formal Regulations

The most important key component of the MCMV-E model is, first of all, the entity itself. How is it defined, how does it relate to other institutional actors, and how does it operate within the formal guidelines of the program, and what are those specifically?

The entities are the social or judicial bodies of joint families functioning in self-organized autonomy over transferred public resources and over design and self-management of the construction process. The entity can thereby assume different legal forms, such as social housing associations, NGOs, co-operatives, or social housing movements. Among them, only the collective construction phase can be considered to follow the co-operative model, since substantial co-op conditions are missing, such as collective ownership or continuation of the co-op entity after completion of the project.

There are essentially three ways to constitute a social housing entity. First, an already established entity might deliberately select the families for project-specific application of MCMV-E funds. Second, families may approach an entity and subscribe to waiting lists for the next application round, or self-motivated families and members gather to form an entirely new entity. Once it fulfills the necessary prerequisites defined by the Ministry of Cities, the entity receives permission to apply for the program and act as formal representative of all inscribed members.

The Ministry of Cities regulates and controls the program guidelines and procedures. The employment, however, is managed by the operating agent, the federally controlled savings bank Caixa Econômica Federal. Local offices of the bank receive the direct application from the entities and approve or deny funding after valuation. At that point, the processing is fully decentralized. The relationship between entities and local officers turns out to be crucial, for they become direct contact persons for mutual negotiations. There are strong divergences in regard to these relationships, ranging from harmonious to adversarial. Some local agencies are inclined to cooperate with the entities for successful implementation of the minor model within the MCMV program, offering social-technical assistance, workshops, or precise application guidelines to facilitate access to the program funds. In many cases, however, a distant relationship is observed, hindering a fluid process and blocking developmental social proposals. There are great differences also in the normative interpretation of the overall program guidelines. Innovative proposals might be welcome by some agencies, while others won't accept original typological concepts.[11] We encounter discretionary powers and arbitrary decisions on the operational level, especially because the final evaluation for funding approval is met solely by financial agents and not by qualified officials with knowledge of inclusive urban sustainability.

Once the application for MCMV-E funds is approved, the access to land is the next great challenge encountered by the entities. The MCMV program encourages purchases from private landowners. For that aim, loans are transferred in anticipation of guaranteeing an effective acquisition modality. But without qualitative regulations regarding strategic urban locations for the MCMV-E projects and only a low price limit clearly stated, the result is evident: 2 percent of the projects are located in the city's central area, 68 percent are in peripheral areas, and around 30 percent are within the urban expansion belt.[12] The creation of satellite settlements generally represents one of the major detrimental results of the federal program, which unfortunately didn't manage to define differentiated regulations for the MCMV-E model. Given that the program has already secured access to land from private agents, the local state and municipal authorities show little interest in allocating public land to social entities. What's more, local managers are no longer willing to develop their own urban instruments, such as development plans combined with property rights and land-use policies. In this regard, the development of local urban policies, strongly motivated by the Ministry of Cities in its initial phase, came fully to a halt, while the quantitative MCMV federal program also replaced the qualitative communication between federal and municipal authorities. In opposition, most entities adopted a rather pragmatic and militant approach in trying to negotiate public land donations. In order to avoid state or municipal resistance, some entities opted for direct negotiation over vacant public buildings or land belonging to the federal government. Some prominent entities organized impactful initiatives rendering desirable results in central areas, such as the entity Utopia e Luta (Utopia and Fight) in Porto Alegre and the Manoel Congo occupation in Rio de Janeiro.[13] Most of the 2 percent of central cases managed to negotiate exceptional public land donations. Despite being successful prototypical examples, the low statistics demonstrate that this approach is still far from becoming the feasible norm. Here again, the few examples rather represent the spirit of militant perseverance, standing for the potential of democratic capacity building in contrast to the programmatic pattern.

Another major difference between the commercial and the entity models of MCMV is the self-management of design methods and construction mechanisms. In self-managed construction schemes (self-construction by the beneficiaries, self-help, mutual assistance, and direct management) the organizing entity, together with the families, manages the entire project construction, following the tradition of the Mutirão construction co-operatives of the 1980s. Several forms were tested, applied, and observed in the MCMV-E model. Examples range from self-build, hiring only specialized labor, to the "global contract" modality, which allows the organizing entity to delegate the entire building process to a construction company. This approach highlights a possible partnership between entity and small-scale constructors of regional character. Given the smaller size of the construction companies, the organizers emphasize the possibility of greater control and monitoring by the families, the flexibility to elaborate the project, and the possibility of adopting a larger range of construction systems.[14] The participatory factor doesn't necessarily decrease but is rather redirected into experimentation with different forms of management. Strategies for construction vary and have not been sufficiently systematized. The entities mobilize different conceptions and forms of construction regimes, organization of the construction site, market formation, and accountability, among other mechanisms, which is precisely the core of the debate on self-management of housing and city production. The best practice examples of successful MCMV-E projects display a high level of efficiency in combining and applying those different mechanisms to attain the most productive yet participatory results.

The participation of qualified social-technical assistance was a crucial factor for the integral success of the few well-implemented MCMV-E projects. The multidisciplinary relationship between the entities and technical-assistance agencies fosters significant social-technical capacity building and innovative solutions, which generally are difficult to achieve within the rigid formal guidelines of the program. Innovative attempts require arduous, persuasive discussions with the operating agents Caixa Econômica Federal, since experiments outside the narrow framing of the program rules are consistently rejected. Since the Mutirão experience in São Paulo, social-technical assistance has become one of the most important elements for efficacious, innovative, self-managed housing solutions.[15] The most productive technical-assistance agencies are mostly engaged in the metropolitan areas of the state capitals. They matured during decades of experience within the context of micro-political self-organization, which makes them more efficient and qualified than ever nowadays. Elsewhere throughout the country, on the other hand, the professionalization of technical-assistance agencies is still extremely undeveloped, creating regional discrepancies. Since the Ministry of Cities distanced itself from the urban reform agenda, the federal investments in the formation of technical assistance in smaller communities has stopped. Another factor hindering the development of a balanced technical-assistance system is the lack of an educational background in participatory planning of self-managed social housing production, since this subject requires complex systemic study of multidisciplinary areas, such as architecture and urban planning, engineering, social service, social and human sciences, and law, among others. The academic curriculum of architectural education hardly considers that broad scope. Lastly, the pragmatic, most ponderous explanation for the precariousness of a well-functioning technical-assistance network is related to the program's framing itself. Technical-assistant agents begin the service without any previous financing. The horizon for a project to be contracted or approved is unknown, and can last several years in some cases. The initial unremunerated support can't be afforded by small agencies. This impacts the performance of the entities, which often renounce the service of technical-assistance agents altogether, favoring simplistic market typologies that can be rapidly and pragmatically implemented to solve the pressing needs of the families. A low diversification of housing models and lack of innovation is therefore the clear overall picture of the program, unfortunately also in the MCMV-E modality.

High Performance of Capacity Building despite Insurmountable Restrictions

Despite the difficulties, it is still possible to point out stunning MCMV-E cases, among them, for instance, the MCMV-E Florestan Fernandes e José Maria Amaral in São Paulo, which was completed in a mutual self-help modality (Mutirão) in 2018. The complex was fully built and organized by joint efforts of the large social movement Movimento dos Trabalhadores Sem Terra Leste 1 (Landless Workers' Movement), the technical-assistance agency Ambiente Arquitetura, which has existed since 1992 and is one the most active and successful in the country, and around 400 engaged families. The challenging high-rise typology was implemented within four years of full-time self-managed construction. The rapid pace of negotiations and the well-organized mobilization process were only made possible because of the high level of capacity building and social leadership skills acquired after decades of militant experience and micro-political engagement. Best practice examples as such show clearly what can still be achieved by the effective alliance between entities, families, and technical assistance, revealing the major difference between the two models: namely the social capacity building that enables the group to collectively surmount the unfavorable programmatic setups of the inflexible MCMV program. Since the MCMV program was never designed to accommodate the need for micro-political, social development, the mere integration of the participative model can already be seen as a great micro-political accomplishment, fully represented by such examples.

However, the general program follows an altogether different intention, which is the mass production and mass consumption of housing as a publicly financed commodity with almost negative use value. Cheap access to housing was massively generated, indeed. But the MCMV program also generated mono-functional satellite cities, drastically obstructing sustainable urban growth. Apart from severe urban disintegration, the market-oriented solution fails to offer any social-technical innovation for social housing concepts. As a result, the urban texture remains predominantly organized by the uneven development between self-organized, unregulated urban spaces and the over-engagement of the private sector, aggravating segregation and increasing adversarial socio-spatial urban geographies. The movements did initially secure 5 percent of the MCMV program budgeted to subsidize co-operative housing production, of which only 1.5 percent could be successfully employed.[16] It isn't nearly enough to tackle social-spatial segregation and the spread of urban enclaves that are being intensified through the massive MCMV program guidelines.[17] Although the participative approach contains key elements designed to cope with such urban challenges, the program doesn't allow the co-operative benefits to fully unfold.

Although the MCMV program today stands in drastic contrast to the initial intentions of the original sustainable urban policy goals, the successful implementation of the original multilayered policy transformation depended on a larger systemic, political, and economic master plan that considers the urban fabric as a compound result of cross-systemic references to qualitatively tackle the enormous present housing deficit of the country, as well as to remediate decades of neglect of the issue. Such a complex master plan has been attempted and developed since the 1990s. The determination of democratic social movements since the 1980s led to macro-political policy strategies that could have engendered the necessary breakthrough for an authentically democratic and inclusive urban policy. The long-term course for such systemic transformations required collective political and social capacity building, which fully evolved and manifested over two decades, materializing the foundational structure for adequate visible urban recovery to take place. In last instance, however, decades of focal, micro-political efforts towards social and professional capacity building were co-opted by macroeconomic pressure and macro-political compliance, resulting in a program that extracts abundant sources of public capital and utilizes democratic institutions and instruments to reintroduce the same old urban patterns of segregation and dysfunctional generic mass housing solutions seen during the military regime.

Against all odds, the best-practice examples implemented in the MCMV-E modality stand for the utmost effective, professional, and political capacity building to mobilize social-technical and human capital, adapting to extremely unpropitious conditions to enable the emergence of socially sustainable communities within the highly discriminatory rules of the program and the market. Instead of exhausting valuable social capital as hostages of a deficient social housing program, the vital question is now how to institutionally reorganize and utilize the highly developed political and social capacity of civil movements to obtain basic independence from macro-political confinement. Perhaps the answer is already present in the core of the approach, which has been focused on cooperation since the very beginning. The full development of micro-political resistance, which is best supported by co-operative models, may allow the movements to regain strength in order to reformulate strong social micro-political claims and to fight forcefully again for their authentic, macro-political implementation.

1 Mutual self-help co-ops, as described in detail in the article "The Mutirão Program: Co-operative Housing Production Intersecting Micro- and Macro-political Spheres," pages 79–92 in this book.

2 The original manifest of the **Reforma Urbana**, a paper once formulated in the early 1960s, became a term coined to define sustainable, inclusive urban policy goals. See N. G. Bonduki, **A luta pela reforma urbana no Brasil: Do seminário de habitação e reforma urbana ao plano diretor de São Paulo** (São Paulo: Instituto Casa da Cidade, 2018).

3 Brazil's National Urban Policy of the 21st Century is explained in detail in N. G. Bonduki and A. P. Koury, **Os pioneiros da habitação social** (São Paulo, Editora Unesp; Edições Sesc, 2012), 108.

4 See E. Maricato, **Brasil, Cidadades: Alternativas Para a Crise Urbana** (Rio de Janeiro: Editora Vozes, 2011).

5 Public investments in the housing sector grew from 5 billion reals in 2005 to 18 billion in 2008, while private investments ranged from 6 to 25 billions in the same time window. The joint private and public invested capital grew from 11 billion

to 43 billion. Bonduki and Koury, **Os pioneiros da habitação social**, 117.

6 During the next years, the PT-guided SNH developed the PlanHab, a consistent long-term national urban policy plan to be implemented until 2023, based on the reform agenda. From this plan only the high subsidy capacity funds FNHIS was applied in the MCMV program, neglecting the qualitative principles defined by PlanHab. See ibid.

7 Ibid.

8 The Ministry of Finance proposed 270,000 units. Lula suggested one million units with a focus on low-income families for the first phase of MCMV. See R. Rolnik, **Urban Warfare: Housing under the Empire of Finance** ((London: Verso, 2018).

9 Ibid.

10 The PlanHab policy strategy was based on the consistent survey of the accumulated and future housing deficit, concluding a total deficit of 34.9 million units, conducted by the SNH in 2007 and 2008. Bonduki and Koury, **Os pioneiros da habitação social**, 116.

11 Research on social housing undertaken by the research network FINEP in E. Burguière, F. H. Ghilardi, J. P. Oliveira Huguenin, S. Kokudai, and V. da Silva, **Produção social da moradia no Brasil: Panorama recente e trilhas para práticas autogestionárias** (Rio de Janeiro: Letra Capital, 2016).

12 Ibid. Statistics of represented MCMV-E projects are included in the survey.

13 Ibid.

14 Ibid.

15 See the role of social-technical assistance as described in detail in the article "The Mutirão Program: Co-operative Housing Production Intersecting Micro- and Macro-political Spheres" in this book.

16 In comparions, 61,600 units of MCMV-E settlements were contracted until 2017. In 2018, the total budget cut for MCMV-E occurred, while 3.9 million units of MCMV commercial were contracted until 2018. **Subsídios e Subvenções da União—Valores Pagos—Subvenção Econômica ao Programa Minha Casa Minha Vida**, Ministerios das Cidades, 2018.

17 R. Rolnik et al., "O Programa Minha Casa Minha Vida nas regiões metropolitanas de São Paulo e Campinas: Aspectos socioespaciais e segregação," **Cadernos Metrópole** 17, no. 33 (May 2015).

Co-operative Capital: Making Use of Collective Micro-fund Models for Housing Production

Sascha Delz

Integrating the low-income population and the lower middle class into credit and housing markets has been a major challenge in the postwar era — both in industrialized and developing contexts. While the middle classes and upper-income groups have had relatively easy access to loan products through specifically tailored financial products and public policy incentives, the bottom third of the income curve has usually had difficulties in conforming with the rather strict lending frameworks. In response to these deficits, the "formal" market has primarily focused on establishing a microfinance industry that provides loans at a scale and for conditions that are more favorable for the respective beneficiaries. The "informal" market, on the other hand, has always produced financing mechanisms that enable citizens to get access to small amounts of capital for more favorable and flexible terms. Having access to such funds is a key feature for housing production in less wealthy contexts, not only because people usually do not dispose of large amounts of cash or savings, but also because, as a result, housing construction commonly happens on an incremental basis. Looking at one of the most popular practices, the rotating savings and credit associations (ROSCAs) model, is an illustrative example for how capital can be pooled, accumulated, and distributed on a co-operative and nonprofit-oriented basis. This model is especially prevalent in Africa. Looking at the Ethiopian version of a ROSCA — namely the Iqqub — on the one hand, and focusing on more inclusive ways of housing finance, on the other hand, illustrates scenarios of how the Iqqub concept could be conflated more effectively with co-operative housing production: using the established structures of collectively leveraging micro-funds, the Iqqub idea could generate capital at various levels and scales of co-operative housing production. Moreover, apart from these rather direct funding proposals for housing production, the way ROSCAs and Iqqubs are structured ultimately allows for an understanding of the creation and accumulation of capital on other terms.

The resulting "co-operative capital" represents a version of capital that is not solely a market commodity detached from physical production on the ground but an inherently social construct that inseparably connects democratic, co-operative production processes and livelihoods with the creation of capital.

Microfinance: Promises and Challenges

Expanding access to financial services and loan products to a broader part of populations has been one of the main challenges and efforts of mainstream economic development policies in the postwar era. The common goal behind these efforts, bluntly, is to promote the two main aspects that are considered essential for the dominating neoclassical economic engine of growth: creating savings and stimulating investments. In this system, the story goes, a larger amount of the population can undertake growth-oriented investments by leveraging accumulated savings through loans, which — if profitable – increase savings that can be invested again, and so on. Yet, while a variety of governmental tools and policies — specific loan products, incentives, tax reductions for starting businesses or buying houses, etc. — have been established for making the middle classes part of these growth cycles, including the lowest income groups in such credit schemes has been more difficult. This is particularly the case for the poorest citizens of developing countries: in many places, setting up state-controlled, subsidized credit schemes for the lower income groups — as it was established for the middle classes of industrialized countries — was often not sustainable.[1]

The failure of such loan schemes under the then-dominant development policies led to a substantial shift in perspective during the 1970s and 1980s. Breaking with the public sector by focusing on the private market, and offering smaller units of credit rather than commonly sized loan products tailored for the middle class, gave rise to what we know today as the microfinance industry.[2] Equally important, initial microfinance schemes changed other fundamental characteristics of common banking practices as well: for the Bangladeshi microcredit pioneer Muhammad Yunus and his Garmeen Bank, for example, microfinance was conceptualized as a nonprofit undertaking to help people out of poverty by focusing on human and economic development at the same time. Accordingly, this approach not only entailed lower credit rates for beneficiaries but also established other ways of lending, controlling, and securing collaterals. Or in other words: the original innovation made by the Garmeen Bank and other early microfinancing actors "was not just the idea of lending to the poor at more reasonable rates. It was figuring out *how* to do it."[3]

Unsurprisingly, tapping the gained knowledge of how to more effectively lend to the poor, microfinance has since grown into a global industry where NGOs and nonprofits are joined by commercial banks, global investors, and financial markets to compete for clients.[4] Although originally based on a nonprofit idea and simultaneous human and economic development, microfinance has become a commercial business where the "social" aspect is usually reduced to the aspect of social control to secure payments rather than social development as a whole. As one of the most vocal critics of this development, Ananya Roy, accordingly states: "The globalization of microfinance has generated great interest in microfinance as an 'asset class,' or as a circuit of investment. While the Garmeen Bank promises to alleviate poverty and empower women through a nonprofit model of financial services, new models of microfinance institute strict norms of financial sustainability and emphasize profits rather than human development."[5] As a result, microfinance has covered a wide spectrum of lending practices but has also displayed conflicting positions. Roy summarizes this dilemma as "neoliberal populism," where "microfinance seeks to democratize capital and simultaneously convert the micro-capital of the poor into new global financial flows."[6] She accordingly asks the fundamental question: "Will the poor benefit from such integration or will their inclusion take place in highly exploitative and predatory ways?"[7] Because for her, "the promise of microfinance, of its democratization of capital, is that the idea and practice is more widely owned, that we can all participate in it."[8]

Yet, when looking at so-called developing contexts, the challenge of gaining access to loans and financial services has sparked many other ways and schemes of micro-funding that are not profit-driven, co-operative in nature, and thus primarily focused on the needs of its members or immediate communities. Accordingly, if we leave aside the more recently institutionalized meaning of the term "microfinance," small-scale financing schemes have naturally been part of everyday lives for a long time. Besides the almost inevitable emergence of money sharks and lenders who take advantage of the population's desperate monetary needs, people have also pro-actively collaborated to meet their financial necessities by more co-operative manners. While in more affluent countries or societal groups such efforts often result in co-operative banking practices such as credit unions or mutual banks, the poorest citizens usually have to side-track such "formal" arrangements and create their own financing mechanisms that work outside official banking regulations. On the African continent, for instance, "the most popular instruments are rotating savings and credit associations (ROSCAs) — more commonly known as 'merry-go-rounds' in English-speaking Africa and as *tontines* in Francophone countries."[9]

An illustrative example of such a ROSCA scheme is the Ethiopian version called Iqqub (or Ekub). Following the overall idea of a ROSCA, an Iqqub "is a savings association where each member agrees to pay periodically a small sum into a common pool so that each, in rotation, can receive one large sum."[10] Any group of people can cooperate to form an Iqqub association, define the sum to be paid regularly, and determine the organizational and fiscal arrangements. In its most basic form, an Iqqub's running cycle is determined by the amount of people participating. After the last member has received the full sum, the Iqqub can be dissolved or renewed.[11] A further characteristic of the Iqqub is that it is deeply rooted in people's everyday lives, because it "is based on pre-established social ties. It consists of homogeneous groups: people from the same work place, ethnic background, trade, schooling background or neighborhood. People from all walks of life, ranging from the rural poor to the urban rich, from shoe-shine boys to high level government officials, participate in the Iqqub."[12] The "pre-established social ties" are also the main control mechanism: usually, a group of Iqqub participants guarantees for either each other or a new member. If a member cannot pay the requested amount per cycle, the guarantors are responsible for coming up with the missing funds.

The way Iqqubs — and ROSCAs in general, for that matter — are structured results in a highly hybridized setup that can hardly be covered by a "formal" bank: when participating in an Iqqub, every member is debtor, creditor and beneficiary at some point in time. Combining these preexisting social ties with the co-operative nature of an Iqqub association, the hybridity establishes a rather particular setup where the rotating fund's members strongly depend on each other as a group in order to generate funds for every individual. Furthermore, unlike traditional banking practices, the mixture of a co-operative setup (nonprofit, run by and for its members) and a hybrid structure (credit and savings tool at the same time) enables the Iqqub to address some of the fundamental challenges Ethiopian low-income groups face when it comes to generating savings on the one hand and accessing loans on the other: while the minimal sums that people can put aside on a regular basis are conventionally not interesting for commercial banks, Iqqubs allow participants to deposit rather small amounts (depending on the members' self-determined aggregates). Whereas commercial banks have to make profit from offered services through fees and interest rates, the nonprofit setup of an Iqqub only charges running costs and does not place a disproportionate additional burden on the participant's finances.[13] Finally, the Iqqub setup effectively means that a prospective Iqqub member does not necessarily have to have assets for collateral as usually requested by banks: theoretically, one can get access to an Iqqub solely via a system of trust that guarantees that he or she can put up the respective money every cycle. Some Iqqubs even permit that several people can join to pay for one quota, meaning that the threshold to participate can be substantially lowered by pooling even smaller funds.

In summary, Iqqubs enable members to transform small parts of their income into savings and loans in ways they are usually not able to do with the general microfinance sector — let alone with the common banking industry. Two main aspects make Iqqubs distinctly different and thus valuable alternatives to conventional microfinancing frameworks. First, considering that in today's microfinance sector nonprofit versions — such as the Garmeen Bank— are a minority, the Iqqubs' intrinsic co-operative and participatory structure does not generate profits for individual members or the Iqqub as a whole. This makes them truly nonprofit entities from the outset and basically protects them from being taken over by a profit-making scheme. Second, Iqqubs overcome common banking relations: even when looking at nonprofit microfinance institutions, there is still a classical relation between lenders and recipients, where the bank defines the lending conditions, enforcements, and sanctions while the beneficiary is obliged to follow the given framework. In a co-operatively organized Iqqub, however, all the functions that are normally defined by a bank are decided and carried out by the collective of participants. Thus, in combination with the Iqqubs' possibilities to include almost every income group, one could argue that Iqqubs are indeed performing a "democratization of capital" which nearly "all can participate in," to reiterate Ananya Roy's idealistic demand for microfinance in general.

Housing Finance: Conventional Mortgages versus Incremental Construction

Now what could a ROSCA's features imply for the production of affordable and adequate housing? Conventional formal housing developments are usually defined by two main characteristics. On the one hand, the built structures — buildings and housing units — are principally conceived as turn-key projects, meaning that the prospective owner or tenant moves into a finished home. On the other hand, turn-key homes are typically financed by a credit system — namely the mortgage market — that is designed for and built on using the housing project as collateral. This means that in this system, buildings and their respective finance mechanisms are rather inflexible: the house is a finished product that has to be paid off with a strictly laid out financial plan — the mortgage. This creates a framework of mutual enforcement, where a specific way of building a house is inseparable from its related financing mechanism, and vice versa. In fact, the Ethiopian government has, like many other countries, tried to cope with housing shortages and rising construction costs by starting a low-cost housing program based on a mortgage system in 2004, building thousands of subsidized, ready-made units in standardized housing blocks.[14]

Yet, for most low-income groups — as with lending, savings, and spending — housing usually happens in small steps and in small pieces. A house usually reflects the owner's momentary status of family, income, and savings, which results in dwellings that, from a banker's, planner's, or government official's point of view, are not finished and might never be finished at all. As Abhijit Banerjee and Esther Duflo point out, a finished house in these contexts is the rule rather than the exception, because "if you ask owners why they keep an unfinished house, they generally have a simple answer: this is how they save."[15] Banerjee and Duflo illustrate this exemplarily along Banerjee's own family experience: "When Abhijit's grandfather earned some extra cash, he would add a room to the house. … Abhijit's family used to have a driver who would occasionally ask for a day's leave. He would buy a sack of cement, a sack of sand, and a stack of bricks and would take a day off to lay some brick. His house was built over many years, 100 bricks at a time."[16] Clearly, a typical mortgage market is not able to address such incremental building processes. But a microfinancial scheme can. It is within this realm of housing production where a ROSCA such as the Iqqub can be of great value for its beneficiaries: as with a classic microfinance loan, the typical amount of money generated through an Iqqub can contribute to an incremental construction process and finance specific housing parts such as a roof, a kitchen, windows, etc. However, while typical microfinance products leverage their customers' incomes through credit by creating debt for the borrowers and income for the lenders via interest rates,

Iqqubs can leverage small amounts of income without a down payment and without creating long-term debt or excessive additional spending due to interest rates.

Co-operative Capital: A Collective Way to Leverage Income for Housing Production

But what if the Iqqub scheme is taken beyond its conventional boundaries? What potentials could be unlocked, for instance, if Iqqubs were specifically integrated into, and tailored for, co-operative housing production? In this way, the Iqqub concept could not only help provide nonprofit funds for individual investments for specific building parts, but could also be used as a co-operative practice that provides capital for large-scale and long-term investments needed for whole housing projects. In adapting the Iqqub framework towards co-operative housing production, three different levels addressing different scales could be considered.

At an *individual level*, similar to a conventional setup, the Iqqub could provide capital for individuals to finance certain items or investments. But instead of leaving it completely open to the members to decide what to buy with the rotating funds, there could be a coordinated effort that specifically directs the collected money towards housing parts within a respective housing co-operative. For example, an "individual housing Iqqub" could have the objective of raising money for windows and doors. Starting with this common goal, there would still be different ways of implementing it. The resulting funds could, for instance, be put aside for the whole Iqqub cycle to then order a larger batch of windows and doors and get better offers from producers. Or, the co-operative could decide that the rotating fund is disbursed after every cycle — as in a conventional Iqqub — but with the direction that these funds have to be used for doors and windows. In this scenario, the individual members would still have a certain freedom to choose the product, producer, or even buy their own materials and help build the items themselves.

At a *collective level*, the Iqqub members could pool their rotating funds to build up or extend collective aspects of a co-operative organization. This "collective housing Iqqub," would be probably the most helpful at the very beginning of establishing a housing co-operative: the Iqqub's financial leverage could be used, for instance, to raise the needed capital to start or run a housing co-operative, enabling Iqqub members to pay their initial shares and thus start to build up the co-operative's capital stock. Again, while there might be a common directive for the raised capital's usage, the members could still determine the details of arrangements, amounts, modalities, etc.

Finally, at a *co-operative level*, the Iqqub system could be scaled up to the whole housing co-operative. Collaborating among co-operatives, each co-operative would represent one member and thus be the beneficiary of the rotating fund. The "co-operative housing Iqqub" would also offer different modalities for how to spend the rotating funds. At a basic level, of course, every co-operative could individually decide on where to invest its capital — such as acquiring new land, building basic housing structures and green spaces, or investing in renovations or upgrades. But they could also collectively agree to pool resources and direct them towards mutual interests. If there are a couple of neighboring co-operatives, for example, they could invest into common infrastructure or additional land. Or if the co-operatives are spread all over the city, they could collaborate to use the rotating funds to purchase construction materials in bulk. Clearly, all these Iqqub iterations could be complementary — or be the entry point — to more institutionalized co-operative financing tools offered by, for example, co-operative or mutual banks.

Apart from these scenarios in which Iqqubs could be directly applied to co-operative housing production, the Iqqub approach also bears a more systemic and transformative potential. As mentioned above, a classical mortgage or microfinance system usually puts responsibility entirely on single individuals or households, ideally creating savings and profits in the long run for its beneficiaries, but also resulting in dependency and vulnerability by aggregating all risk to the smallest units of a society. This is rather ordinary within the current economic system, where capital has essentially become a tradeable commodity through which one can make as much individual profit as possible. ROSCAs and Iqqubs, on the other hand, are not only participatory nonprofit schemes that pool risk among its participants: the hybridity of their members' simultaneous roles as creditors, debtors, and beneficiaries creates rather different relation between the realms of capital and society. Through these kinds of co-operative processes, the accumulation of capital becomes an inseparable part of everyday practices, of social life, and — in the case of housing — of urban production. By adding an inherently social and collective dimension to money, this sort of "co-operative capital" could not only be an essential agent that can create alternative possibilities to gather, pool, and accumulate funds on a nonprofit basis for co-operative housing practices but could also be a more general starting point to transform the waywe understand capital from a micro-political and thus more democratic perspective.

1 For complex and more detailed reasons why the poor do not or cannot lend from official credit institutions, see, for example: Abhijit Vinayak Banerjee and Esther Duflo, **Poor Economics: A Radical Rethinking of the Way to Fight Global Poverty** (New York: PublicAffairs, 2011), 157–81.
2 See, for example, Joanna Ledgerwood, **Microfinance Handbook: An Institutional and Financial Perspective** (Washington, DC: World Bank, 2000), 1–3.
3 Banerjee and Duflo, **Poor Economics,** 166.
4 Ananya Roy, **Poverty Capital: Microfinance and the Making of Development** (Oxon: Routledge, 2010), 5.
5 Ibid., 5.
6 Ibid., 32.
7 Ibid., 32.
8 Ibid., 32.
9 Banerjee and Duflo, **Poor Economics**, 186. See also Daphne Frank, **Sustainable Housing Finance for Low-Income Groups: A Comparative Study** (Baden-Baden: Nomos, 2008), 48.
10 Dejene Aredo, AERC Research Paper 21, **The Informal and Semi-Informal Financial Sectors of Ethiopia: A Study of the Iqqub, Iddir, and Savings and Credit Co-operatives** (Nairobi: African Economic Research Consortium, 1993), 9.
11 For more detailed and fine-tuned Iqqub setups regarding credit, lottery alterations, etc., see, for example, Arnaldo Mauri, **The Role of Financial Intermediation in the Mobilisation and Allocation of Household Savings in Ethiopia: Interlinks between Organized and Informal Circuits** (Milan: Fondazione Giordano Dell'Amore, 1987), 8–11.
12 Aredo, **Informal and Semi-informal Financial Sectors of Ethiopia**, 11.
13 See Mauri, **Role of Financial Intermediation**, 11–13.
14 For more information on the program, see for example, UN-Habitat, **Condominium Housing in Ethiopia: The Integrated Housing Development Program** (Nairobi: United Nations Human Settlements Programme, 2011).
15 Banerjee and Duflo, **Poor Economics**, 183.
16 Ibid.

The Mietshäuser Syndikat: A Structural Answer to Anti-speculative and Self-Governed Housing Production

Anna Heilgemeir

A crucial factor hindering many affordable housing projects in recent decades is the speculation-driven increase in land prices that make affordable rents nearly impossible to realize. The Mietshäuser Syndikat (Tenements Trust) offers a response to this crisis by questioning the underlying mechanisms of such speculative markets. The Mietshäuser Syndikat is a self-governed organization that was founded in Germany with one initial project in the early 1990s, and now consists of over 140 housing estates of different sizes located all over the country.[1] As an alliance of diverse interest groups, the model offers a path towards structural change of ownership and governance in the housing sector by countering trends of privatization and breaking the prevalent logic of speculation.

An Operational Idea for Housing Owned by Its Tenants

The main innovation developed by the Mietshäuser Syndikat concerns the restructuring of established forms of homeownership. To guard housing projects against speculation, each building that belongs to the Mietshäuser Syndikat features a model of divided ownership: every housing project is owned by a limited liability company (Haus GmbH), which – in turn – is owned by two shareholders, the Hausverein (Dwellers' Association) and the Mietshäuser Syndikat. The syndicate itself is a nonprofit limited liability company that consists of, and is owned by, an association formed by the inhabitants of all Mietshäuser Syndikat houses in Germany. While the structure of the limited liability company allows the Hausverein to be self-sufficient in all questions concerning the use and management of the house, the Mietshäuser Syndikat has the mandate to safeguard the ownership status of a building and to prevent the property from privatization. In essence, the Syndicate model is a type of trust that splits the traditional property status of real estate into two parts: control over the utility value, which can be determined by the tenants, and control over the capital value, which is determined by the syndicate's nationwide association.

A further important principle of the syndicate addresses finances. Tenants finance the house through so-called *Direktkredite* — small private loans with low interest rates — from people in the wider network as well as additional credits from banks that are paid off via rents.[2] This means that the future inhabitants' ability to finance their homes is basically independent from their personal financial resources. Once the house is paid off, tenants maintain the house through rent payments while other projects can be supported with the solidarity fund. The solidarity fund is another crucial aspect of the Mietshäuser Syndikat: it is used for public relations, payments for infrastructural costs, and as the original deposit for the syndicate's share in each new Haus GmbH. In case of urgent financing shortfalls, the solidarity fund can be used to provide credits as well.[3]

The Mietshäuser Syndikat's origins can be dated back to 1983, when a project group called Grether-Baukooperative für Instandsetzung in Selbsthilfe (Grether Building Co-operative for Repair in Self-Help) was founded in the German city of Freiburg. The Grether co-operative was formed as an answer to the demand for political support from another housing project in jeopardy, thereby raising the question of whether efforts in solidarity should be directly connected to permanently safeguarding common goals. This engagement ultimately led to the idea of transforming single housing projects into a housing and solidarity network founded on collective goals, where the respective groups of inhabitants could make their own decisions for and about their houses. As a result, the Mietshäuser in Selbstverwaltung (Tenements of Self-Organization) was founded in 1992, and was renamed Mietshäuser Syndikat in 1993.[4] Between 1996 and 2001, seven projects in southern Germany joined the movement, with the first one established outside the federal state of Baden-Württemberg in 2001.

Against the backdrop of conflicts emerging from an increasing housing shortage and rising land prices, the Mietshäuser Syndikat model has more recently become an important tool to counter speculative interests in Berlin's housing market. In view of the model's capacity to join opposing forces of bottom-up movements and top-down structures for the common good, the following examination of aspects of Berlin's housing history will briefly focus on the achievements and shortcomings of both private and public actors and will attempt to show the potential and role that the Mietshäuser Syndikat could have for a more comprehensive and progressive vision of affordable, collective housing production.

A Brief History of Housing in Berlin: Impulses for Sociopolitical Change and the Challenge to Implement Sustainable Long-Term Strategies

Looking back at some aspects of the last thirty years of Berlin's planning history, a few relevant points outline a well-intentioned but often unsustainable cooperation between self-organized appropriation and state action. In the 1980s, the housing sector of West Berlin was strongly influenced by a squatter movement that claimed empty and abandoned buildings in the center of the city in an attempt to alleviate the housing shortages in the "formal" public and private sectors. At the time, around 200 buildings in West Berlin were squatted. Unlike other radical political groups, the alternative, left-leaning squatters' movement was supported by a large number of bottom-up neighborhood initiatives. Even the church claimed housing as a right, protesting against urban renewal and protecting the run-down building substance of the well-known, mid-nineteenth-century typology of the so-called Berlin block as a flexible, mixed-use structure. This broad solidarity combined with persistent public pressure — exemplified through repeated street protests and demonstrations[5] — ultimately not only resulted in a public subsidy system that supported the repair of houses through self-help but also institutionalized the squatters' practice of *Instandsetzung* (repair and modernization during occupation). Eventually, nearly half of the squatted buildings were reconditioned by their inhabitants and were legalized along the way with subsidies from the government's newly installed framework Behutsame Stadterneuerung (Careful Urban Regeneration).[6]

Although through this support the squatter movement's ability to reclaim the use value of housing ultimately led to a flourishing revival of communal housing practices and shared living models — such as raising children in larger social groups, "open door" principles, common hallways and kitchens, self-managed companies and alternative production, neighborhood shops, social organizations like *Kitas* (self-managed day-care centers) — the state's subsidies did not secure any long-term goals for equitable housing production. When it came to ownership models, for instance, political financing strategies rarely developed structures that would expand collective property rights; rather, these schemes often enabled the transformation towards private ownership.[7] As a consequence, hundreds of housing estates remained in either private or public hands at the risk of becoming part of a growing real estate asset that could be sold for profit after a certain period of time. And this is exactly what happened to many housing estates in Berlin's center during the following two decades.

Market Integration of Self-Governed Projects and the Sale of Public Land and Housing Assets

With the fall of the Berlin Wall, the city's housing and real estate market experienced a massive influx of more affluent private actors on the one hand and larger profit-oriented investors on the other. For these actors, Berlin's land was cheap, and the newcomers from former West Germany, Europe, and the rest of the world entered the city to develop their own living and investment models. Almost at the same time (particularly from the mid-1990s on) — and after two decades of supporting former squats and self-managed housing through the of Behutsame Stadterneuerung program — the ruling conservative CDU (Christian Democratic Union) party started to enforce the law called Berliner Linie, which allowed the city to clear newly established squats within 24 hours. This dwindling political support for the squatter movement and self-managed housing models, combined with a period of fast development and transformation triggered by new financial investments and interests, put the alternative nonprofit housing scene in dire straits.

Within this climate, the focus of funding policy for self-managed structures started to shift from collectively managed, politically left-leaning projects to the so-called *Baugruppen* in the mid-2000s. Baugruppen are collectively managed models for housing investment and development that are based on private ownership and that have been mainly established by members of the middle class who often have privileged access to land and financial resources.[8] Regrettably, questions concerning the surrounding neighborhoods, social structures, accessibility for the many, social responsibility, affordability, and long-term tenure security were not usually an integral part of these projects. As a result, projects of collective housing at that time were mainly a part of the Baugruppen model that — although often resulting in experimental, free, changeable, variable housing typologies — usually required a shared class background, shared political orientation, as well as an agreement on supporting private profit within the project.

In the meantime, the state had largely withdrawn from financing construction of public housing, mainly due to the need to fill financial gaps and a simultaneous trust in the private market to provide the needed housing stock. Consistent with this strategy, the city of Berlin additionally sold around 1,600 hectares of public land as well as whole public housing blocks between 2001 and 2012. Finally, most of the public housing companies were privatized to fill the holes in the city's budget.[9] Although officially everyone who wanted to invest or buy was cordially invited to do so, the traditional nonprofit actors such as self-managed housing groups, co-operatives, and public housing companies were not specifically supported in buying or developing land, and it wasn't particularly in their interest to do so at that time, since there appeared to be still enough open space in the city and rents were generally still affordable. However, many of the former squats and self-managed housing projects that were not already part of models like the Mietshäuser Syndikat became part of two processes during this period: on the one hand, former squatters somewhat supported an increasingly unfair distribution of space — it was not uncommon, for instance, for one person to live in a 100 m² flat with rent far beneath the city's average — on the other hand, some of the remaining members of former squatter groups contributed to the trend of privatization by selling their buildings — usually with substantial profits — thereby adding to the dynamics of the speculative housing market.

Fighting for Affordable Nonprofit Housing and the Transformation of Housing from Property to Belonging

Against the backdrop of rising rents and disappearing land resources in favor of private housing projects, a new wave of protests from the early 2010s on started to demand a more just and affordable housing delivery system as well as to preserve the remaining open spaces for the common good: the initiative Media Spree Versenken! (Sink Media Spree!) started with a campaign and a referendum against the commercial riverside development Media Spree;[10] a Round Table for Public Land Politics[11] was founded to promote change in land politics and the halt of privatization; bottom-up tenant associations such as Kotti+Co and Sozialmieter.de co-organized protests against the rising rents for public social housing; and in 2014, the referendum Initiative 100% Tempelhof successfully campaigned to keep the runway field of the former inner-city airport of Berlin open and free from housing construction driven by real estate investors or middle class housing co-operatives.[12]

This protest movement of various social groups, tenant organizations, and neighborhood initiatives was not only born from the realization that daily lives were increasingly put in danger by plain displacement or unaffordable rents. The movement also fought for the rights of belonging, namely the right and need to appropriate and actively shape living environments through collective action and participation. With this perspective of belonging, many initiatives simultaneously started to consolidate their protest and claims into concrete proposals and solutions, which introduced a whole new discourse on why, how, where, and by whom affordable housing developments could be realized. With a rather narrow field of options to achieve concrete results in this regard, more and more of these bottom-up groups considered learning from the Mietshäuser Syndikat model. Yet, while the syndicate's approach could secure the basic claims for collective organization, participation, and nonprofit housing, it still depended on the availability and affordability of land resources or already built housing structures. Meanwhile, backed by a broad support within civil society, the new protest movement appeared to have triggered a slow, yet visible, paradigm shift within governmental authorities as well. Moving away from the positions that land is still seen as an asset to be privatized, and of giving Baugruppen and large-scale private investors preferential access to remaining land resources, the movement has started to force the city government to change strategies regarding the allocation of public land as well as how to set up cooperation frameworks between public housing companies and bottom-up nonprofit housing initiatives. Combining and integrating these efforts with the Mietshäuser Syndikat model, for instance, could potentially open a whole new perspective on the role and meaning of the Mietshäuser Syndikat. Going beyond self-managed individual housing estates, the Mietshäuser Syndikat could become part of a much more open, comprehensive, common, and accessible understanding of affordable nonprofit housing practices.

A Pragmatic Approach for Leveraging Collective, Nonprofit, Affordable Ownership beyond Co-operative and Public Housing

In view of the failures of both individually and collectively owned housing schemes to alleviate the pressing housing crisis, the need for housing models that not only halt speculation but also offer financial power and secure long-term stability — without abandoning self-determination of its tenants — appears obvious. The combination and integration of the syndicate idea into the described efforts from civil society could open a whole new perspective on the role and meaning of the Mietshäuser Syndikat within a city's affordable housing policies.

As mentioned above, the Mietshäuser Syndikat already takes a crucial step towards a new conception of what collective ownership of a housing estate could mean: by breaking apart utility value from capital value, the model safeguards the property from speculation. As the brief tale of Berlin's alternative housing movements shows, however, the ability to create affordable housing is not only dependent on protecting housing estates from purely speculative activities — in fact, both co-operative and public housing schemes can suspend speculation. But there are dominant challenges directly related to speculation that are not in the control of such organizations, regardless of their existing speculation-free housing stocks: within a rising speculative market, it becomes more and more difficult for nonprofit actors to acquire additional land or properties and thus expand accessibility to land and financial resources for more people. Even when assuming that a large co-operative, for example, could afford respective prices, generating widespread access to affordable housing remains an issue: because of their strong — and important — rootedness in their respective communities, co-operatives essentially cater to their members and often do not cross city boundaries.

The scope of the Mietshäuser Syndikat, on the other hand, is different. Although it consists of an aggregation of rather small housing estates, it is geographically limitless and can, theoretically, be scaled endlessly. Because of its twofold collective ownership structure, it is part of a national organization and can draw from a much larger and constantly growing network. It is here where the Mietshäuser Syndikat could become a driver of yet another new understanding of what ownership is and means: while the syndicate's collective financial leverage would allow to act like a large investor to finance acquisitions of a substantial amount of land and property, the syndicate's collective values could further leverage the provision of affordable housing and thus expand access to housing beyond particular organizational or geographical memberships that are linked to most co-operatives or public housing schemes. Finally, the syndicate offers the crucial element of long-term stability. When joining the syndicate, the ownership structure makes sure that the building will remain within the affordable nonprofit housing stock in the long run. Again, since one half of each of the respective estates is owned by the nationwide network, local or individual interests cannot change the general nonprofit and collective status of ownership.

Sharing Knowledge and Translating the Mietshäuser Syndikat System to Other Countries

From a global perspective, Germany's particular challenge in providing affordable housing has been part of a worldwide trend of rising rents, the withdrawal of the public hand, and privatization and displacement processes within the housing sector. It is therefore of no surprise that since its inception, the Mietshäuser Syndikat has received many inquiries from groups abroad who wish to build on the syndicate's example in their own countries. And through its inherently collective, nonprofit setup, the syndicate has naturally shared its knowledge and resources where possible. However, while it is possible to transfer the system in principle, each country faces different challenges, such as various approaches to ownership, different judicial, economic, and tax systems, or different economic situations of the population. In essence, the Mietshäuser Syndikat describes the main challenge as follows: "Every group from a different country that wants to establish a syndicate-like model is faced with the same tasks as the small group from Freiburg in the early 1990s: How do you defy an economic system that is geared to maximizing profits by developing a model that works for our ideas of a good life for all—in which effort and benefit are in reasonable proportion?" [13]

Despite these difficulties, organizations such as Le CLIP, Vrij Coop, and habiTAT have been established to work on comparable models in France, the Netherlands and Austria. Although they all build on the same general principle, each describes their respective aims differently: Le CLIP defines its goal as creating "an archipelago of places in ownership of use";[14] Vrij Coop's intent is to found "an association of housing co-operatives that strives for affordable housing for everyone, where a house is not a tradable object, but a place to live together";[15] and habiTAT's manifesto states "that alternatives to the real estate market are created that make beautiful living possible regardless of the financial background," and "that all people have the right to independently organized housing" where "your children may already have the choice between the constraints of the real estate market and self-initiated, self-managed forms of housing."[16] Besides mainly working on the basis of volunteer work or crowdfunding, these initiatives and organizations are also supported by the German Mietshäuser Syndikat network, which through its nonprofit statutes and collective values naturally sees such actors rather as allies than competitors. Here, a large part of assistance is the development of locally adapted legal forms and sample rental agreements. Other important components — often in order to acquire any houses and properties at all — are lobbying, strategy development for public relations, and political campaign management.

Setting Up Mutually Beneficial Regulations and Support between Bottom-up and Top-Down Structures

Regardless of the various models and leverages that nonprofit housing actors such as the Mietshäuser Syndikat apply to prevent housing from becoming an asset within a speculative market, the mere price levels of land resulting from these speculative activities still make it difficult for such entities to acquire land and start a project in the first place. In many cases, the only way to get access to affordable land is to make use of favorable regulatory powers that city governments and state actors have over certain parts of their territories. This means that even for an officially autonomous organization like the Mietshäuser Syndikat, legislative support from city and state actors becomes an important part of starting a housing project. In this regard, top-down political-support measures such as subsidies, advantageous building regulations, the assignment of public land to dependable self-governed structures (including co-operatives), and the support of self-governance as an alternative applicable to public housing construction are of great relevance.

Furthermore, since housing projects built by initiatives such as the Mietshäuser Syndikat often appear to be small-scale initiatives that only serve a limited amount of people,[17] a collaboration between self-help initiatives and state actors could become particularly relevant in times of immense shortages of affordable housing: What role can bottom-up initiatives such as the Mietshäuser Syndikat play in alleviating these issues in cooperation with top-down governance structures? How can they be scaled up? How can they be made accessible to a more substantial part of society? What is their relationship to public housing, and can beneficial elements be replicated in the public sector? Is a mixture of systems possible? And what can we learn from the past?

In Germany, and particularly in Berlin, these questions are finally part of a rising public discourse on topics that surround issues such as the general relation between self-governed projects and municipal housing, the link between land appropriation through joint processes and official planning frameworks, and the proportion between freedom for self-chosen ways of life and societal equality beyond the scope of individual cases.[18] In an attempt to understand the city in general, and housing in particular, as a common good within contemporary urban development, the articulation of these relationships will become increasingly important.

1 Mietshäuser Syndikat, accessed fall 2019, https://www.syndikat.org/de/.

2 Small loans are usually between 500 and 10,000 euros, sometimes larger. The smaller the loans given, the more stable the financing will be. If a small loan expires, a new lender can easier be found. Some projects are financed with more than 100 small loans. Interest rates can be chosen between 0 and 3 percent.

3 Using the Solidarity Transfer as a credit line is, however, rather rare; see https://www.syndikat.org/en/solidarity_transfer/.

4 Sabine Horlitz, "Housing beyond Profit: A Comparison of U.S. and German Alternative Ownership Models," American Institute for Contemporary German Studies, Johns Hopkins University, June 29, 2012, https://www.aicgs.org/publication/housing-beyond-profit-a-comparison-of-u-s-and-german-alternative-ownership-models/.

5 See Berlin Besetzt, http://www.berlin-besetzt.de/#.

6 The principles of Behutsame Stadterneuerung were adopted in 1982 by the Berlin parliament with the pressure of the broad civil society. They contained socially acceptable preservation and user-oriented modernization rules for old building quarters instead of demolition and new construction or suburban developments; see http://www.internationale-bauausstellungen.de/geschichte/1979-1984-87-iba-berlin-die-innenstadt-als-wohnort/12-grundsatze-der-behutsamen-stadterneuerung-ein-paradigmatischer-wandel-in-der-stadtentwicklung/. It is discussed critically in terms of power politics, pacification strategies, and gentrification processes in, for instance, Andrej Holm,

Die Restrukturierung des Raumes: Stadterneuerung der 90er Jahre in Ostberlin: Interessen und Machverhältnisse (Bielefeld: transcript, 2015).

7 The establishment and expansion of common property was therefore encouraged, but was not a prerequisite. At the same time, however, there were also examples of a sustainable promotion policy, such as support for the founding of a co-operative that still exists today, Lusienstadt eG.

8 "Senat will Baugruppen fördern," **Tagesspiegel**, July 10, 2008, https://www.tagesspiegel.de/berlin/bauen-in-berlin-senat-will-baugruppen-foerdern/1276090.html

9 http://www.liegenschaftsfonds.de/fileadmin/user_upload/PDF/Begleittext_Studie.pdf.

10 Initiativkreis Mediaspree versenken!, https://ms-versenken.org/.

11 Initiative StadtNeudenken, https://stadt-neudenken.tumblr.com/Runder%20Tisch; Runder Tisch Liegenschaftpolitik (@TischRunder), Twitter, https://twitter.com/tischrunder?lang=de.

12 100% Tempelhofer Feld, https://thf100.de/start.html.

13 "International Projects," Mietshäuser Syndikat, https://www.syndikat.org/en/international-projects/.

14 "Le CLIP? C'est quoi?," CLIP, http://clip.ouvaton.org/blog/index.php?category/LE-CLIP-C-EST-QUOI.

15 Vrij Coop, https://vrijcoop.org/.

16 "habiTAT Kickstart – solidarisches Wohnen in Österreich," Start Next, https://www.startnext.com/habitat.

17 Horlitz, "Housing beyond Profit."

18 See, for example, Stadt von Unten, www.stadtvonunten.de/stadt-von-unten-selbstverwaltet-und-kommunal-city-from-below-self-managed-and-common/.

Housing the Co-op

Towards Self-Organizing Cities

Co-operative Development Goals: Urbanization Scenarios for Africa between Social and Technological Innovation

Rainer Hehl

If we look at the statistics predicting population growth and urbanization trends for the current century, the next urban revolution will undoubtedly happen in Africa. Outpacing previous development scenarios in speed and scope, the urbanization of the African continent will engender a socio-cultural transformation for which neither the world nor Africa is fully prepared. While at present 15 percent of the world's population is African, the share will increase to 25 percent by 2050 and to above 40 percent by 2100.[1] Compared to the urban revolution of the industrial age, which substantially transformed urban life in Europe and across the globe, Africa has to manage a complex demographic transition from rural to predominantly urban on an unprecedented scale in one-third of the time that it took previously. What is particularly striking is the fact that a major portion of this urbanization process will most likely happen informally — in other words, without sufficient provision of infrastructure and formal housing. If the future of Africa cannot be thought of in neat, ordered modern categories driven by top-down governmental planning and market-led development, what are the alternative scenarios for a continent undergoing massive transformations? At the intersection of demographic, cultural, economic, technological, and political shifts, co-operative practice appears to bear the potential to open imaginaries for alternative urban futures that haven't been sufficiently seized by local and global agencies yet.

If Nigeria's population continues to grow and people move to cities at the current rate, Lagos could become the world's largest metropolis within the next sixty years, home to 85 to 100 million people. Similarly, Niamey, the barely known capital of Niger, a West African country with the highest birthrate in the world, could explode from a city of fewer than one million people today to the world's eighth-largest city, with 46 million people. And Kinshasa is expected to grow from 12 million to 83 million inhabitants. By 2100 the world's population centers will most likely have shifted to Asia and Africa, with only 14 of the 101 largest cities in Europe or the Americas.[2]

What is particularly disturbing for researchers and close observers of urban growth is the fact that African cities are swelling to extensive urban agglomerations that are difficult to govern through state institutions and that do not offer the prospect of sufficient income and adequate shelter. The dramatic mismatch between demographics showing a much larger share of children and youth compared with other regions of the Global South and the formal labor market represents the core problem for future development in sub-Saharan Africa.[3] Youth unemployment is at a record high in the aftermath of the 2008 economic downturn, with little hope of improvement, and the International Labour Organization (ILO) has issued warnings that the majority of this youth will remain trapped in precarious or "vulnerable employment."[4] Informal work status then goes hand in hand with informal dwelling or slum-like living conditions. Slum prevalence affects up to half of the African population, and an even greater portion has to deal with makeshift conditions in a kind of gray zone between formal service delivery provided by the state, formal markets, informal private agents, and place-based collectives. As formal and informal investments shift and recalibrate, these hybrid systems are continually reconfigured, representing the makeshift, adaptive pulse of the city.[5] When urban informality shapes the prevalent mode or "way of life," city building becomes predominantly an organic and quasi-state affair, hinting at vast systems of social organization, exchange, oversight, regulation, violence, reciprocity, and continual recalibration. Thus, urban informality ceases to describe a shadow world beyond state control in favor of what Edgar Pieterse and AbdouMaliq Simone termed "the adaptive city": "Once one accepts that the scale of informality as a mode of urbanization is insurmountable for states in poorer countries, and that urban residents are the primary builders of the city, then our conceptual vocabulary has to shift away from simply accounting for structural drivers of urban inequality to providing an understanding of how things get done amid overlapping and dense social relations."[6]

Given the hybrid character of adaptive urban systems, future scenarios have to be developed on the basis of an understanding of these dense social relations between diverse agents and agencies. But we also have to give up the predefined models that were promoted as examples for good urban governance, promising a compact, mixed-used urban fabric interlaced with ample green public space and a vibrant public life rooted in a growing creative economy that offers abundant opportunities for a newly emerging urban middle class.[7]

What would be an alternative scenario — one that is able to counter the neoliberal development paradigm and that bears the capacity to balance resources to establish the framework for equitable and sustainable development?

As the present picture indicates, the future of the African continent cannot be measured and projected with the same criteria that were applied for the Industrial Revolution. In order to manage a complex demographic transition from rural to predominantly urban in one-third of the time and on an unprecedented scale, the Global South cannot draw on the replication of development strategies from the Northern Hemisphere. This becomes ever more obvious in view of the fact that the upcoming urban transformation in Africa cannot rely on subsidies that allowed imperial powers to extract value and achieve economic dominance, exploiting colonies in the Global South for economic support during the periods of slavery and colonialism. But there is still another aspect that differentiates the current phase from the previous age. According to technology historian Carlota Perez, who has investigated the changing patterns of economy, technology, and governmental policy from the onset of industrialization to the contemporary situation, the full transformative impact of the current information and telecommunication technology (ICT) revolution on society has caused a disruption with former conditions that is profoundly changing the cultural and institutional practices and related development paradigms at stake.[8] For some political analysts this might even result in the end of neoliberal capitalism and in the emergence of a new postcapitalist development model. In any case, the driver for transformative change will no longer be represented by the working class, as "info-capitalism has created a new agent of change in history: the educated and connected human being."[9]

Looking ahead to the forthcoming challenge of urbanization in Africa, a few important questions emerge: Who are these new agents? How are they connected? And more importantly, how will they be educated and trained to enable a better future? A particular case of slum upgrading in South Africa will give insights into how the formation of new agents can come into effect, and what kinds of problems might be encountered on the way.

Skills and Capacities

In the Cape Flats, an expansive, low-lying area situated to the southeast of the central business district of Cape Town, informal dwellers exist in a state of helpless temporariness — helpless, since they don't possess the technical skills to improve their homes, and temporary, because they hope the state will replace their shack with a permanent house.

After the end of apartheid, South Africa established an ambitious Reconstruction and Development Program (RDP) aiming at the implementation of a socioeconomic framework for alleviating poverty and addressing the massive shortcomings in social services. Between 1994, when the program was initiated, and 2014, around 3 million subsidized housing units have been built across the country, but of the estimated 12.5 million South Africans (14 percent of the total population) without proper housing, a large number of people are still waiting for their turn. Similar to the mass housing program Minha Casa Minha Vida in Brazil, the RDP housing program provides basic housing units predominantly based on the single-family type. Even though the RDP houses improve the living standards for dwellers who formerly lived in informal settlements, most of the units are poorly built with repetitive schemes; their planning and layout, designed by large-scale construction companies, is dreary and monotonous — to the extent that they often resemble the bleak building programs of the apartheid regime during the 1950s and 1960s.[10] In some instances, RDP housing delivery led to violent conflicts within communities — corruption is widespread and the units are often incompletely inserted into the overall planning framework. With the attempt to combine measures to boost the economy (such as contained fiscal spending, sustained or lowered taxes, reduction of government debt, and trade liberalization) with socially minded service provisions and infrastructural projects, the RDP program sought to resolve two problems at once — the housing shortage and structural economic deficits — resulting in high unemployment rates. The reality, however, shows that despite enormous efforts to provide formal housing, informality and unemployment are still on the rise in many urban areas. According to figures published by the city of Cape Town in 2018, the metropolitan region saw a 53 percent increase in land invasions. Drastic measurements to expropriate the squatters do not contribute to a solution — instead of containing informal growth, a coherent strategy for upgrading slums and providing infrastructure is urgently needed. In Khayelitsha, the largest township in the Cape Flats and home to about 400,000 dwellers, over 50 percent of the working-age population is unemployed, which makes young people vulnerable to drug abuse and criminal offenses. Seventy percent of the residents still live in shacks, and one in three people has to walk 200 meters or more to access water. Informal shack dwellers are prohibited from using permanent building materials, which leads to an informal market of building materials for temporary shelters, where residents sell used building components, scrap wood, and prefabricated corrugated metal sheets with inbuilt window- and doorframes.

For the social enterprise Hands of Honour, this local market bears the potential to extend business activities. Hands of Honour combines social engagement with business by gathering the unemployed, former drug addicts, and gang members and instructing them in furniture production and the renovation of dilapidated buildings. The initiator and director of the program, Paul Talliard, was trained by a Dutch NGO to set up the business model professionally and to create an internet page for better visibility. The social enterprise, which has already been awarded an international prize for its achievements, is committed to improving the living conditions in the neighborhoods as well as job offers within the local labor market. So what if these newly trained workers deployed their capacities to build houses for underserved populations?

In 2015, Hands of Honour collaborated with architects and engineers on a project aimed at the development of a prototype for an incremental housing scheme.[11] As a result, the workers of Hands of Honour were trained with the help of a local builder to set up a construction system consisting of a low-cost reinforced concrete structure erected with locally available building materials. A piece of infrastructure rather than a building, the so-called table house provides a solid base to start with. The structural frame attempts to address the lack of stability of the informal settlement. Gradual improvement of livelihood hereby offers an appropriate way to progress in view of limited economic means and the availability of materials and their life cycles. By recycling and upcycling existing materials, the construction system initiates new value chains in order to promote a local building economy that ties into local social and cultural practice. It is striking that the overall costs for one unit built in an incremental manner only amounts to one-tenth of the price of a RDP housing unit.

The first table house erected by Hands of Honour challenged governmental policies by deploying permanent building materials within informal conditions, but it also reconfigured current practices of distributing land and subdividing it into individual lots. By multiplying the available building ground and providing a shelf system where multiple housing units can be inserted, the prototype questioned the common practice of turning land into private property. Due to its ambiguous nature, the table house operates in a kind of gray zone between formal and informal practice, and is therefore a thorn in the side of local authorities as it consolidates informality and turns the temporariness of informal dwelling into a permanent status that can no longer be controlled by governmental agencies. But the implementation within illegally erected settlements was also problematic since it was very difficult to cope with the dynamics of informal negotiations that are leading to complex internal power structures, often controlledand manipulated by rivaling gangs operating within local communities.

It was only with the help of a co-operative organization that the table house found a viable common ground, allowing the group to erect the structures legally and without getting involved in complex negotiations of informal tenure status. The Klipfontein Land Trust, a co-operative community organization that holds a lease on land owned by the Methodist Church, saw the incremental building strategy as a viable means of coping with invasions of squatters increasingly occupying available land and threatening the borders of their property. The alliance between community land trust and social entrepreneurs allowed them to set up a scenario for the implementation of a group of structures on the fringe of the community land, serving as a test bed for a densified collective housing structure that can be erected by local builders and improved gradually over time by the inhabitants themselves. Even though the joint partnership represented an exemplary model of co-operative practice for improving technical as well as social skills and for promoting local building practice, the project collaboration reached its limit when it came to the provision of infrastructure for running water, sewage, and electricity. In the end, the "educated and skilled human being" that provides the foundation for a new type of co-operative economy needs more than just mobile devices for enhanced connectivity — he or she also relies on the connection through physical infrastructure provided top-down by governmental agencies. In order to change the current scenario, governmental authorities would have to alter their planning practice significantly in favor of a process of mediation between formal and informal housing provision, emphasizing the development of instruments to enhance local markets, skills, and capacities.

A New Paradigm for Sustainable Growth

The present situation in cities like Cape Town might represent an exemplary case for a possible future scenario in other African countries. Ranking as the second largest African economy after Nigeria, South Africa can be considered much more developed than other economies of the continent that are predominantly driven by informality and lacking urban governance. Even though South Africa might have the capacity to set up necessary infrastructure to develop the country in sustainable and equitable ways, and despite massive efforts to provide subsidized housing for the urban poor, its so-called Gini coefficient, which indicates the level of inequality, is the highest in the world. This clearly indicates that another kind of development goal is needed, one that attempts to balance resources and puts urban dwellers in an active position to develop knowledge and financial capacities for managing housing production on their own. It is clear that in this scenario, social and economic development goes hand in hand. It has already been stated that, considering the described challenges the continent has to face, it is obvious that informal development and self-organization has to be complemented and supported by infrastructure and services provided by state institutions — sustainable growth can only come into effect when people can find work and when the formal economy generates sufficient state funds for governmental investments. The mediation between formal and informal relies on resources and frameworks in order to turn it into a productive force.

Global institutions have started to realize that co-operative forms of organizations are able to combine social and economic development and to assemble the capacity of self-organization present in informal situations with economic models that can operate within the formal market economy. The UN estimated that in 1994 the livelihood of nearly three billion people — or half of the world's population — was made secure by co-operative enterprises. UN-Habitat illustrates the potential of co-operative development with the case of Kenya, where co-operative societies play a significant role in the country's economic growth and co-operative employment creation amounts to 240,000 people and contributes to 45 percent of the gross domestic product.[12] The UN-Habitat publication *The Organization, Management and Evaluation of Housing Cooperatives in Kenya* also states that housing co-operatives have become an essential means of dealing with the challenges of over-urbanization in Kenya, and there has been a mushrooming of microfinancing institutions to enable the formation and sustainability of new housing co-operatives.[13]

However, despite evidence demonstrating that co-operatives can play a major role in a new development paradigm, they haven't been sufficiently promoted by global agencies yet. Urban politics and development agendas actually still seem primarily concentrated on regulating policy for the improvement of top-down governmental structures. Both the United Nations' Sustainable Development Goals (SDGs) agenda, agreed to in September 2015, and the New Urban Agenda, adopted at the Habitat III conference in October 2016, would require a financial and infrastructural revolution to ensure the level of access to housing and basic services that are set as targets through state provision.

While almost all national governments have signed up to the pledges of the SDGs, it seems impossible in the current operating environment of globalized finance systems to raise the requisite capital investment to meet these targets. It is telling that alternative economic models and the promotion of co-operatives are only mentioned in these development agendas to a degree that can be reduced to the significance of a footnote.

Despite lacking coverage, there is evidence that co-operatives are on the rise. If we look into the presentation of the International Co-operative Alliance (ICA), a global network for co-operatives, the extensive scope of this organizational model is illustrated by the fact that more than 12 percent of humanity is part of any of the three million co-operatives in the world, employing 280 million people, which amounts to 10 percent of the world's employed population.[14] However, it seems that here the sectorial organization dealing with housing co-operatives plays rather a minor role within the ICA network. If we look at the mission statement of this global alliance, which claims that "through self-help and empowerment, reinvesting in their communities and concern for well-being of people and the world in which we live, co-operatives nurture a long-term vision for sustainable economic growth, social development and environmental responsibility," we realize that co-operative development exactly matches the ambitions as stated in the SDGs and the New Urban Agenda. So why is co-operative development not yet part of these protocols for joint action?

There are diverse reasons why "business for and by the people" isn't in the foreground for envisioning future scenarios of growth. It might be, in some cases, that co-operative practice still carries ideological connotations, particularly within countries that are marked by a socialist or communist past. More importantly, co-operative development calls for a shift of the present capitalist economic paradigm based on individualization and private property — a shift that still faces massive resistance by a powerful lobby of corporate capital and neoliberal interest groups. Housing co-operatives could play a leading role in changing the development paradigm by countering this resistance. As the housing question is indispensably linked to the question of how we live together and how we can set up the collective project of a neighborhood or a city, it represents the complete scenario for envisioning and creating future livelihoods. Housing production relates to all kind of life cycles — it is investment and energy intense and linked with global flows of resources and human capital — and it impacts to a large extent how far well-being can be achieved through sustainable means.

If we hold this new development paradigm against the present and anticipated challenges for urbanization on the African continent, it is clear that innovation in social organization will be as important as technological progress. In the advent of the information age and the upcoming urban revolution, it is the educated and connected urban dweller who will determine whether future scenarios will take on co-operative and equitable traits. While social and technological development can no longer be dissociated, it is the process of producing and operating in common, rather than predefined housing models and standardization, that should be the target of speculations and investments. Only with an operational mode of how to act collectively will it be possible to develop the 700 billion housing units that are needed for Africa within the next fifty years.

It is curious that the only global organization that numbers co-operative development among its top goals is the ILO, which launched a "Promotion of Co-operatives Recommendation" in 2001 and that meanwhile established its own branch focused on co-operative labor practice. The ILO estimates that 279 million jobs are provided through co-operatives, which represents a significant contribution for promoting decent work and advancing SDGs.[15] In a recent publication, the ILO even demonstrates with the case of agriculture co-operatives in Africa that co-operatives are emerging as critical economic actors in climate-change adaptation and mitigation — from mutual insurance to renewable energy to forestry and waste management.[16] With the slogan "Transforming Our World: A Cooperative 2030," the ILO also states that ten of the seventeen SDGs can be achieved through the promotion of co-operatives.[17] It seems obvious that shelter co-operatives in emerging economies in Africa and other regions of the Global South can play an important role within this equation.

There was a moment when the ILO was already leading for predicting a future scenario for urban development. It was the ILO that first analyzed economic activities outside the formal economy in Kenya in 1972 using the term "informal sector," which had been coined by economist Keith Hart's previous study of economic activity in Ghana. The term "informality" then entered the discourse of urban studies twenty years later, in the 1990s, when it was used to describe the extensive spread of unplanned, self-built urban environments across the globe. Thus, there might be hope that within the next twenty to thirty years, co-operative cities will be as common as informal cities.

1 United Nations, **International Migration Report** (New York: UN-DESA, 2015) www.un.org/en/development/desa/population/migration/publications migrationreport/docs/MigrationReport2015_Highlights.pdf.

2 See Daniel Hoornweg and Kevin Pope, "Population Predictions for the World's Largest Cities in the 21st Century," **Environment and Urbanization** 29, no. 1 (April 2017): 195–216.

3 In Africa, children accounted for 41 percent of the population in 2015 and young persons aged 15 to 24 for 19 percent. Latin America and the Caribbean and Asia, which have seen greater declines in fertility, have smaller percentages of children (26 and 24 percent, respectively) and similar percentages of youth (17 and 16 percent, respectively). In total, these three regions were home to 1.7 billion children and 1.1 billion young people in 2015. United Nations, **International Migration Report**, 7.

4 According to the ILO, stable employment includes wage and salaried employees and business owners. Vulnerable employment includes subsistence farming and work for family members. International Labour Office, **Global Employment Trends for Youth 2013: A Generation at Risk** (Geneva: ILO, 2013).

5 E. Pieterse and A. Simone, **New Urban Worlds: Inhabiting Dissonant Times** (Cambridge: Polity

Press, 2017), 38.
6 Ibid., 39.
7 F. Tonkiss, **Cities by Design: The Social Life of Urban Form** (New York: Polity, 2014).
8 C. Perez, "A Green and Socially Equitable Direction for the ICT Paradigm," Globelics Working Paper Series 2014-01, p. 20.
9 P. Mason, **Why It's Kicking Off Everywhere: The New Global Revolutions** (London: Verso, 2012); P. Mason, **Postcapitalism: A Guide to Our Future** (London: Penguin, 2015).
10 Tom Lodge, "The RDP: Delivery and Performance," in **Politics in South Africa: From Mandela to Mbeki** (Cape Town: David Philip, 2003).
11 The test project was initiated by the Alfred Herrhausen Gesellschaft and coordinated by Jo Noero architects in Cape Town and Rainer Hehl in Berlin.
12 UN-Habitat, **The Organisation Management and Finance of Housing Cooperatives in Kenya** (Nairobi: UN-Habitat, 2010).
13 UN-Habitat, **The Organisation, Management and Evaluation of Housing Co-operatives in Kenya** (Nairobi: UN-Habitat, 2010).
14 "Facts and Figures," ICA, accessed June 17, 2019, http://www.ica.coop/en/cooperatives/facts-and-figures.
15 "Cooperatives," ILO, accessed June 17, 2019, www.ilo.org/global/topics/cooperatives/lang--en/index.htm.
16 "Green and Fair: Cooperatives in Ethiopia," ILO, June 19, 2012, https://www.ilo.org/global/about-the-ilo/newsroom/features/WCMS_183643/lang--en/index.htm.
17 "Transforming Our World: A Cooperative 2030 series," ILO, accessed June 17, 2019, http://www.ilo.org/global/topics/cooperatives/publications/transforming-our-world/lang--en/index.htm.

Shenzhen's Urban Villages: A Micro-political Tale from a China Megacity

Juan Du

China's explosive economic rise in recent decades has generated a global perception of an efficient urban process of state control and top-down planning. From a border town into a megacity within mere decades, the transformation of Shenzhen reinforces such a generalized and monotonous view of contemporary Chinese urbanization. However, hundreds of urbanized villages exist within the city of Shenzhen, each evolved from rural collectives into their current forms of privately held corporations with varying degrees of success. The transformative narratives of Shenzhen's urban villages are unexpected demonstrations of informal networks, self-organization, bottom-up community organizations, and flexible planning and policy-making. Caught within China's drastic sociopolitical and economic shifts, these communities survived and prospered through unprecedented and unexpected multilateral cooperation between individuals and collectives, private corporations and public infrastructure, villages and the city, communities and the state.

Imagine

Imagine a corporation of great wealth. It owns land in the most valuable area of the city's central business district. You saw the directors of the corporation at the mayor's gathering last month. The corporation owns and manages properties while operating subsidiary commercial companies with immense profit. Last year, the corporation's net profit was ¥250 million. Each member received a dividend of ¥50,000, double that of the national average annual income. Children of corporate members go to elite private preparatory schools. A young man recently returned home from the UK with a double degree in business administration and finance, which was supported by a corporate youth scholarship. The elders relax by the koi pond in their lush community garden, sharing vacation photos of their yearly free tours abroad. The latest company newsletter shows the group smiling among cherry blossoms in Japan's Okinawa. The year is 2008.

Imagine a village of great poverty. The villagers are among the poorest in the region, since the land they cultivate is infertile. They have run up such a collective debt that the adjacent village refuses to loan them more money to buy seeds for the next year's crop. Most of the adults have illegally crossed the nearby national border escaping to the world beyond. The children play in groups around the mud-brick homes. They all have swollen bellies that protrude from thin, bony bodies, a sign of extended hunger and serious malnutrition. They are taught to swim at a young age, so that one day they can cross the river and military-patrolled border. There are not many elders in the village, for they perished during the Great Famine more than a decade ago. The year is 1978.

This village became that corporation, all within thirty years.

Huanggang is one of the hundreds of urbanized villages remaining in Shenzhen. The city is the icon of modern China's economic success, where the only detail more incredible than the dramatic socioeconomic transformation is the speed with which it happened, all within mere decades. Huanggang is located near Shenzhen's border with Hong Kong, with a recorded history of over 800 years. In the 1970s, the village was severely — but not exceptionally, by the standards of the time — destitute. From the rural countryside to urban centers, poverty in China was common throughout the 1970s and 1980s. Emerging from the shadows of the three-year Great Famine that caused over thirty million deaths, resources were scarce and strictly controlled by the central government.[1] Then, seemingly in a flash, everything changed. "To get rich is glorious" became a popular slogan that launched China towards its economic turnaround. But what caused this change thirty years ago? How did Huanggang and other agrarian villages transform into the wealthiest societies in the new miracle city? How did China lift 500 million people out of poverty and become the world's second largest economy? The untold tales of Shenzhen's villages shed light on some of the most complex enigmas of China's latest economic and cultural revolution.

Deng Xiaoping, China's premier from 1978 to 1992, is globally credited with single-handedly pitching China towards economic reform. Among other economic reforms, Deng worked for years to convince other politically powerful figures in the central government to open China up to trade with the West. Under pressure to demonstrate his conveniently ambiguous theory of "capitalism with Chinese characteristics," three special economic zones (SEZ) were established in 1980 to cautiously experiment with market reforms.[2] Shenzhen was the first, and most successful, so much so that images of Deng, urbanization, wealth, and Shenzhen were woven together in the Chinese collective consciousness during the formative years of the reform era to inspire further growth. Deng is seen as the founding father of Shenzhen, where he is still affectionately referred to as "Comrade."

To transform China's stale, closed economy, reformers began by learning from China's neighboring free market regions and countries like Hong Kong, Singapore, and Japan that had enjoyed economic success. Reforms to China's economic and institutional policies, such as allowing for private enterprises and foreign joint ventures, were first tested in the SEZs and would catapult the country onto the world stage. The city's rapid emergence was so unexpected and persuasive that nearly all local, national, and international reporting on Shenzhen repeats variations of a similar success story. Such stories appear in the *Shenzhen Daily*, *New York Times*, *Guardian*, and *World Bank Report*: Shenzhen is an instant city with no prior history that was created by a special economic zone which grew at a stunning speed thanks to central planning. "A sleepy village that became a metropolis overnight," has become a new legend of miraculous creation, breathlessly reported around the world. Yet forty years ago, there were nearly 2,000 farming and fishing villages in the territory that became Shenzhen.[3]

Over time, the myth of Shenzhen has only become a more powerful tool for social and political mobilization. Shenzhen is not only viewed as a pioneer and precedent of China's urbanization, it has also become a global model for national governments. From India to Africa to Latin America, developing countries look to China, and specifically to Shenzhen, as a model for rapid economic success that maintains governmental control. Most new megacities of the Global South are struggling with complex socioeconomic problems associated with explosive industrialization and urbanization. The most visible sign of such growth is the prevalence of informal settlements: rural migrants flocking to developing regional economic centers means that municipal governments are unable to keep up with the escalating demand of affordable housing and other public amenities. According to UN-Habitat, more than thirty percent of the urban population of developing countries lives in slums, and this number is only growing.[4] Meanwhile, Shenzhen's rate of urbanization and population growth during the past thirty years is both unparalleled and unprecedented. According to the latest Shenzhen statistical yearbook, in 2017 the city's "non-registered" population reached 8.18 million, compared to only 4.35 million "registered" residents.[5] However, the actual "non-registered" or "floating population" far exceeds the governmental statistics, with estimates placing the actual total population at well over twenty million. Yet outwardly it seems Shenzhen, as well as the rest of China's urban centers, does not have many of the prevalent problems faced by other rapidly developing countries. The speed and apparent stability of Shenzhen's rise in the past thirty years has rendered the city an ideal model for many of these nations. So how was this "Shenzhen speed" possible? And how are there no slums?

The history of China's urbanization in the twentieth century is multifaceted. The myth of Shenzhen must be confronted, for the sanitized image of Shenzhen as a "just add water" instant city is misleading to those imitating the city's apparent success. China has slums, and Shenzhen has the most number of people living in them out of all cities in China. Except they are not referred to or categorically defined as slums, rather they are called *cheng-zhong-cun*, or "villages in the city." The story of the villages and the story of the city are one.

Exclusion and Inclusion

On a cold December day in 1979, a group of strangers visited Huanggang's village head to broadcast the government's decision to build a modern city on the village's land. Not given much of a choice, the residents turned over 90 percent of their ancestral land for a small monetary compensation. They did, however, successfully negotiate for extra trees to be planted on their hillside. But within a year, the trees were uprooted, the hills flattened, and large factory sheds surrounded the village, now reduced to a fraction of its original land. Meanwhile, on the otherwise colorful master plan of Shenzhen, the planners carefully drew perimeters around Huanggang and all the other villages in the city, forming islands of exclusion. The roads, factories, housing, parks, and even power and water supply for the new city were all cautiously built to circumvent the villages. The dirt road that outlined Huanggang would eventually become a high-speed motorway. Starting in the 2000s, gleaming skyscrapers of luxury residences and high-tech towers quickly took over the land previously occupied by 1980s-era factory sheds. The factories, along with the pre-industrialization orchards and hills, became distant memories. The city became a national and international hub for industry and commerce. Domestic vacationers visit the city today for its various theme parks, while others cross the international border from Hong Kong to take advantage of its designer knockoffs and cheap spas.

Meanwhile, due to their rural residency status, villagers were not entitled to the municipal welfare provisions designated for the city's urban residents and had to be self-sufficient. Huanggang, now a collective corporation, joined the new industry of city making. With the meager compensation originally given for their land, in the early 1980s the villagers invested in a truck to haul building material to the construction sites around them and set up small production factories in their historical communal spaces. In addition, each male resident received a square plot of land of 120 square meters on which to build a family house. Women were expected to marry land-owning members of other villages. As there were simply not enough beds at the nearby factory dormitories, migrant workers speaking different regional dialects from all over China soon came to the village to rent rooms.[6] Within the first decade of the new city, Huanggang, as with other villages inside the Shenzhen SEZ, became a vibrant urban center.

As the years went by, villagers began demolishing their homes in favor of taller buildings to accommodate the demand for space from a growing population of migrant workers. These newly built constructions violated the city's zoning codes, so the villagers banded together to defy governmental orders of demolition and defray the risk of fines. The villagers saw this as a way to continue their livelihood. Instead of growing crops, the villagers grew buildings, and in turn became "slumlords." Defying planning and building regulations, many of these buildings grew to fill the entire perimeter of their plot. They were built so close together that they garnered names such as "handshake" or "kissing" towers. Over 50,000 renters eventually came to live among the original 2,000 villagers in the 592 self-built farmhouses.[7] Surrounded by the planned urban fabric, this enclave of otherness, like other villages throughout Shenzhen, became known as an "urban village."

Today, the term "urbanized village" is perhaps more appropriate to describe these types of places, but it still pales in the face of their hyper-dense and urbane realities. There are currently nearly 1,000 urbanized villages (320 administrative villages) remaining in Shenzhen.[8] With profits from rental properties, industrial production, and, later, real estate speculation, the original villagers have become extremely wealthy. The city enriched the villages, and the villages enabled the city. Each urban village is comprised of mixed-income neighborhoods with low- to middle-income renters, all packed into dense housing of varying qualities. Illegally built housing in Shenzhen's urban villages collectively provide shelter to 60 percent of the city's current population on only 10 percent of the city's land.[9]

The Myths of Shenzhen

Shenzhen's centralized urban planning and subsequent deployment of infrastructure was unable to provide sufficient basic amenities such as housing or schools for such an unprecedented population growth. The "sleepy villages" in the repeated tales of Shenzhen were forced to make up for the city's deficiencies. The continued relevance of Shenzhen's urbanized villages today contradicts the accepted theories of its planning success. The textbook formula of the special economic zone superimposed onto a virgin green field, led by central planning, multiplied by "Shenzhen speed" to generate an outcome of a successful mega-instant city – this is nothing but a series of myths. The mythmakers, some intentionally, others fortuitously, have generated a history of the city that strips away much of its nuance, along with the conflicts, ingenuity, and contributions of the original villagers and Shenzhen's millions of migrant residents

The myths surrounding Shenzhen have always served political agendas in China. As a singularly successful case of urban planning, the Shenzhen experiment conveniently sweeps aside the unsightly existence of hundreds of ghost cities – new developments of innovative housing, attractive museums, and lush parks that remain completely empty of occupants and devoid of life – that have also been planned and built over the past thirty years. The most recent central policies plan to continue the country's path of economic growth through urbanization and new town creation. Over the next five years, 100 million rural residents will be urbanized. Hundreds of new cities are planned and currently under construction. In a recent survey of city planning of 156 major cities in China, 145 have plans either to extend themselves or to build new towns. The planned population of these new cities would double the current urban population.[10] The myths of Shenzhen reinforce an assumption that cities can be politically planned and socially engineered from scratch.

Recently issued policies in Shenzhen demonstrate a shift in governmental attitudes towards urban villages: there is a willingness to explore "integrated rehabilitation" rather than total demolition and redevelopment into high-end urban compounds.[11] However, critical questions of "rehabilitation" leading to gentrification that indirectly results in the displacement of low-income residents remain to be answered. Increasingly facing competition from other ambitious cities, Shenzhen must now keep pace with economic growth forecasts to maintain its role as a pioneer city. Anything less than the expected yearly 10 percent GDP growth is viewed as an economic decline. With nearly no land left to attract industries and investment, the valuable pieces of earth underneath the urbanized villages are seen as the last reserves of centrally located land to be developed. The government, in tandem with private developers, is negotiating compensation for villages' remaining properties, but today compensation is based on market value and often includes real estate in the seductively planned development, and villagers are largely complying. The millions of renters, however, have no space at the negotiation table. The most affordable housing stock for the working population will disappear, along with its buildings, neighborly communities, social capital, and network capacities, all of which are intrinsic qualities that have eluded so many well-intentioned social housing and urban development projects around the world.

Like a runaway train, China has modernized and urbanized with such a stunning velocity that there has been little time to reflect on those that have fallen — or been pushed — onto the tracks. Urbanization has been China's most important vehicle for economic growth, and according to the most recent central policies, will continue to be for decades to come. However, the country's rising GDP is rivaled by the hidden costs and disturbing consequences such as socioeconomic inequality and environmental degradation, and the story of Shenzhen's villages is the most intense and buoyant of them all. Thrown into an unprecedented situation, the villages, in becoming the city, have shown remarkable social and economic ingenuity. Contrary to the notions of a generic and instant city, it is the spatial, political, and cultural histories of the urbanized villages — both contemporary and ancient — that define Shenzhen's past and future.

This article has been developed from an earlier version published in **e-flux Architecture**, April 27, 2018.

1 Xin Meng, Nancy Qian, and Pierre Yared, "The Institutional Causes of China's Great Famine, 1959-1961," **Review of Economic Studies**, no. 82 (2015): 1568–611.
2 Mee Kam Ng, "City Profile: Shenzhen," **Cities** 20, no. 6 (2003): 429–41.
3 Juan Du, "Back to the Future: Urban Design Informed by Shenzhen's Hidden Rural History," in **Shenzhen: From Factory of the World to World City**, ed. Linda Vlassenrood (Amsterdam: nai010 Publishers, 2016), 70–91.
4 UN-Habitat, **Slum Almanac 2015/2016: Tracking Improvement in the Lives of Slum Dwellers** (Nairobi: UNON, Publishing Services Section, 2016).
5 Shenzhen Statistics Bureau & NBS Survey Office in Shenzhen, **Shenzhen Statistical Yearbook, 2018** (Beijing: China Statistics Press, 2018).
6 Juan Du, "History of Shenzhen and the Formation of Urban Villages," **Urban Environment Design** 108, no. 8 (2017): 26–31.
7 Fei Chen, "Pengchengyan: Feiyue Huanggang Cun Xishu Sanshi-Nian hou de Tuibian" (The eyes of Shenzhen: Great change of Huanggang village in the past thirty years), **Shenzhen News Net**, 2017.
8 Yaqian Sun, "Shenzhen Chengzhongcun: Cong Dachai - Dajian dao Zonghe Zhengzhi" (Urban villages in Shenzhen: From whole demolition and reconstruction to integrated rehabilitation), **Southern Metropolis Daily**, SA01, May 28, 2019.
9 Ibid.
10 Tie Li and Yi Fan, "Xincheng Xinqu Jianshe Xianzhuang Diaocha he Sikao" (Investigation and reflection on the current situation of new town new area construction in China), **Zhongguo Chengshi Zhongxin (Urban Center of China)**, 2016.
11 Shenzhen Bureau of Planning & Natural Resources, "Shenzhen Urban Village (Old Village) Master Plan for Integrated Rehabilitation (2019–2025)," **Shen Guihua Ziyuan**, no. 104 (2019).

Co-op City: Utopia and Pragmatism in Zurich's Co-operative Housing

Irina Davidovici

In Zurich, co-operative housing is a respected, popular institution with an important history that has linked utopian and innovative thinking with the pragmatic needs of providing adequate and affordable housing. An exceptionally evolved partnership between the local government and co-operatives has enshrined planning culture and regulations as a mutually beneficial democratic model in the city's history. Since the 1920s, this mutual relationship has placed co-operatives at the forefront of providing adequate and affordable housing for Zurich's citizens both in times of prosperity and in times of housing shortages and crises. In a city where dwellings are a contested commodity with an occupancy rate of almost 100 percent, for instance, speculative development is held in check by regulations that ask to preemptively lease available city sites to co-operatives. Furthermore, the grassroots processes inherent in the co-operative model have spurred an ongoing discourse on housing needs from the bottom up rather than being dictated from above. Since the 1990s, this discussion has been invigorated by a group of new co-operatives: merging innovative and pragmatic demands, the projects discussed in the following show the immense potential if political vision and bottom-up social organizations are combined with architectural and urban design ambition. Irina Davidovici describes how this integral setup has enabled Zurich's co-operatives to embrace utopian aspirations and meet pragmatic needs at the same time, showing that innovation and the provision of affordable housing do not have to be mutually exclusive.

A Win-Win Model

Originally established by progressive middle-class circles at the turn of the twentieth century, housing co-operatives acquired a critical mass after 1918, a few years after being adopted by trade unions and large swathes of the working classes. In alliance with the city's social-democratic governance, the co-operative movement shaped entire new districts near the main manufacturing centers, developing large perimeter blocks in Aussersihl and Industriequartier and village-like *Siedlungen* in the neighboring countryside of Wollishofen during the 1920s and 1930s. Following Zurich's annexation of suburban communes in 1934, co-operative housing mainly took the form of the latter, with low-rise flats with pitch roofs and gardens, as seen in the development of Schwamendingen in the 1940s and 1950s. Most of Zurich's co-operative housing to date was built at the time, and it still conforms to a decidedly Fordist model for nuclear families of working men and housewives. Currently, the number of co-operative dwellings is the third largest after that of market rental and private ownership, amounting to a fifth of the total housing stock. This proportion is set to grow further in the next decades as the current strategies of densification target the historical co-operatives.

The major role of co-operatives in the local housing sector illustrates a collectivist spirit intrinsic to Swiss culture.[1] By definition, co-operatives are nonprofit housing providers that secure up-to-date, hygienic, and affordable dwellings to members from every walk of life, without seeking profit or engaging in business speculation.[2] Profits are reinvested as shared capital that helps maintain the housing stock, cater to the needs of inhabitants, and repay loans. As opposed to the largely passive occupants of social housing in many welfare settings, in Zurich co-operative communities count as active and vocal shareholders making full use of their protection and voting rights. The co-operatives' social infrastructure of communal activities and support benefits the wider community, an alignment of interests that marks their success as a form of economic and social organization.

The city's economic and demographic growth since the late 1990s has given the co-operative movement an alternative direction and a new lease of life. Many of the large urban structures built since the late 1990s — from Kraftwerk 1 and Kalkbreite to Mehr als Wohnen and Zollstrasse — were developed by newly established co-operatives who actualize and reenergize the agendas of the original collective actors.[3] Ideologically, these newer co-operatives are indebted to the squatting and youth protest movements of 1968 and the 1980s, reflecting their environmental and anti-capitalist concerns. Their designs therefore aim to implement agendas of citizen participation, communal living, and environmental sustainability, combining housing with civic and commercial facilities, such as urban gardening and common canteens, and promoting alternative forms of collective living in experimental dwelling typologies. The system is flexible enough to allow for significant variations in the size, structure, and underlying ideology of co-operatives, and established enough to remain open to criticism and periodic revision.

Co-operative as Self-Defense

Sociopolitical and ethical subtexts are the foundation of co-operatives, but not a prerequisite for their long-term functioning. Besides their members' well-being, co-operatives are required to ensure their economic survival as businesses — a dilemma that has been a source of inner contradictions throughout their history. The oldest housing co-operative (ZBS: Zürcher Bau und Spargennossenschaft) was founded out of a defensive impulse. In 1892, a group of like-minded individuals from a mostly middle-class background pooled resources in order "to save up and build" their own homes, creating a protective safeguard against speculative housing.[4] As Zurich's population almost tripled between 1880 and 1920, the growing political support for co-operative developments coincided with their being rooted in increasingly utopian ideologies. In this relatively fluid model, reformers could experiment with new means of social organization: Bergdörfli (1914), Zurich's first garden-city settlement, was conceived as an escape from the morass of the industrial city. Still, its inhabitants belonged to an avant-garde professional bourgeoisie rather than the working classes scraping a living in the industrial *Mietskasernen*.[5] The co-operative phenomenon became a grassroot movement with the foundation of the BEP (Baugenossenschaft des eidgenössischen Personals, or Co-operative of Federal Employees) in 1910 and ABZ (Allgemeine Baugenossenschaft Zürich, or Zurich's General Housing Co-operative) in 1914 both self-organized by and catering to laborers. The contemporaneous concept of "housing colonies" — working-class estates conceived as "oases" of a better society — signals an important but familiar aspect of early public housing.[6]

Still, here as elsewhere in Europe, the project of housing the working classes was primarily undertaken by the professional middle classes. By projecting their own values and societal visions of how the laboring classes should live, the policy makers, reformers, and architects involved in the design and procurement of dwellings effected a "culture transfer amounting to a cultural colonisation."[7] In the case of Zurich, the systematic implementation of collective housing types during the 1920s mainly took two forms: the suburban garden-city model of cottages with individual gardens, and the inner-city model of residential perimeter blocks with an internal planted courtyard. In many cases, modernist layouts were concealed under *Heimatstil* roofs and shuttered windows in the attempt to appease various political struggles between the city and the canton. Whether progressive or traditionalist in their architecture, early co-operative developments were socially experimental, setting forth utopian versions of a functioning society. By the 1940s and 1950s, however, when over half of Zurich's co-operative stock was built, pragmatic concerns had largely overridden these ideological ones. In the postwar decades the critical mass of co-operatives lent itself to the purchase of private, ready-built developments, a commercialization that represented a point of ideological surrender.

From Squatting to Housing

The revival of co-operative housing in the closing decades of the twentieth century came unexpectedly from a politicized form of communal living: the squat. Its strong ideological background stemmed from anti-bourgeois, anti-imperialist, New Age, and feminist principles. The occupation of the Globus Provisorium in June 1968 started a trend that continued in the early 1970s with sustained attempts to create autonomous communes.

What was on the surface a generational conflict highlighted the consequences — social, economic, and spatial — of Zurich's transition to a global city. Younger generations felt repressed and marginalized in the conservative and parochial milieu. The May 1980 riots, provoked by the city's decision to refurbish the Opera House while ignoring growing demands for a youth center, marked a turning point in the political consciousness of a new generation.

In parallel, squatting developed from a form of protest into a marginal mode of collective living.[8] The short-lived squat at Stauffacher (1984), on the border between the city's banking area and the working-class district of Aussersihl, was among the most conspicuously anarchic and politically contentious. After the police moved in to clear it, the squatters reorganized into the collective Karthago am Stauffacher, which aimed to convert an entire urban block into a politically autonomous enclave. This utopian attempt articulated for the first time the idea of agency through design, shattering the existing urban order and replacing its conventional typologies with a free-flowing, autonomous entity in collective ownership. The Stauffacher squat and Karthago urban intervention were both theoretically underpinned by the 1983 pamphlet *bolo'bolo*, written under the pseudonym "P.M." by Stauffacher activist Hans Widmer.[9] P.M. envisaged a global network of nonhierarchical, self-sufficient communes called *bolos*, conceived as "extended households" of a few hundred people. These bolos were large enough to allow for the efficient sharing of resources, yet small enough for effective communication and the personal involvement of participants in communal matters. Loosely based on the imagery of tribal settlements, bolos were defined by size and function, while their specific configurations, location, ideology, and cultural identity remained open.[10] Theoretically, this formal indeterminacy enabled intentional communes to emerge and take over existing structures in any city, as well as build new ones. P.M. quipped that with any luck, "*bolo'bolo* can be realized by 1987."[11]

By the time of the second edition, published in 1993, P.M. voiced the more realistic possibility that "under present conditions bolos could be founded in the legal form of co-operatives."[12] Following in the footsteps of Wogeno, this strategy for creating real-life bolo settlements injected new life into the co-operative model. Karthago registered as a bona fide co-operative in 1991, setting up a fifty-strong multigenerational collective household with shared accommodation, catering, and communal duties. The local action group Dreieck similarly opted for the co-operative format to acquire an urban block in order to save it from being torn down. Militant and vocal, these co-ops were effective in reaching their goals in piecemeal fashion, mostly inhabiting existing buildings and thus remaining virtually invisible in terms of design. The use of architecture as a vehicle for alternative lifestyles, inhabiting innovative residential typologies, occurred in subsequent co-operative developments: Kraftwerk 1 (est. 1995), Kalkbreite (est. 2006), and Mehr als Wohnen (est. 2007).

Pioneer: Kraftwerk 1 Hardturm, 1998–2001

The first explicit attempt to bring the bolo theory into practice originated in 1993 with the brochure *Kraftwerk 1*, written and published by P.M. in collaboration with architect Andreas Hofer and artist Martin Blum. Their proposal presented the idea of a live-work collective on a decommissioned industrial site on Zurich's "rustbelt."[13] Reformulating the utopian ideals of the bolo in almost feasible terms, the brochure brought together a collective of like-minded individuals in a series of workshops and cultural events, which culminated with a design brief and the foundation of the Kraftwerk 1 co-operative in 1995. Its first development at Hardturmstrasse was, paradoxically, an offshoot of the economic crisis of the 1990s. The site, recently acquired by the development corporation Allreal, was set aside for a commercial development designed by Stücheli Architects. The lack of market demand allowed Kraftwerk 1 to propose in its place a live-work, mostly residential development, built to high environmental standards.

The detail design was subcontracted by Stücheli to the younger practice Bünzli Courvoisier.[14] Despite being one of the first projects to adopt Minergie standards in construction and environmental performance, the scheme's most experimental aspect nevertheless lies in the layout and variation of apartment types. These ranged in size from studios and conventional two-to-four-bedroom apartments to larger dwellings for collective living. Two *rues intérieures* served a mixture of interlocking family flats and maisonettes (referred to as “Le Corbusier-type”) and these collective units, which featured small bedrooms and shared kitchen and living space (“Loos-type”). Integrating modernist references to distinguish between nuclear family apartments and more flexible collective arrangements points to the role of the architecture in articulating the ideological agenda of the co-operative. Besides its 91 apartments, the ensemble contained a kindergarten, workshops, live-work units, guest rooms, a communal hall and roof terrace, bar, canteen, launderette, and a food shop. A commercial block for offices, with a public restaurant to the street, created a buffer between the courtyard and the road.

Kraftwerk 1 became the leading prototype for the communitarian and environmentalist ideas of the squatters movement. In terms of design, the feedback on the collective flats was used in other schemes and subsequently theorized as a default type for singles and elderly co-operative accommodation.[15] It pioneered a participative consultation process that is now widely used to develop the program of new co-operative developments. Kraftwerk’s success instilled political and financial trust in the validity of ideas — and people — originating from the social periphery of the sqatters movement.

Consolidator: Kalkbreite, 2009–2014

If Kraftwerk started as a manifesto in search of a site, the Kalkbreite co-operative originated from its prominent location in Aussersihl. Despite its proximity to Karthago and Dreieck, this multistory commercial, cultural, and residential complex is as far from these self-effacing beacons of radical living as it is from conventional social housing. What looks like a large urban block is raised above a covered tram depot, hidden from view by a frontage of commercial units at street level: an arthouse cinema, restaurant, bar, stores, and offices. Their mixture of sustainability and commercial appeal feeds the area’s ongoing gentrification.

The overlap of residential, commercial, and transport functions, with the idiosyncratic integration of a heritage building and tram depot, indicate the multiplicity of interests on the site. Earmarked for affordable housing redevelopment since 1978, the parcel was the focus of decades-long debates, which eventually led to a compromise between the local steering group (Kalkbreite Association), the city, and its subsidiary, the public transport company VBZ. In 2006, through its campaign "Ein Neues Stück Stadt" (A new piece of the city), the Kalkbreite Association secured the site lease, and in 2007 it registered as a co-operative in order to carry out the building project. An architecture competition followed in 2009 with 55 entries, most of them from practices in Zurich. The winning scheme, by Müller Sigrist, proposed the assured urban solution of a polygonal perimeter superblock: an inward-looking fortress with a porous public base. The organizing device of the residential zone is a sky-lit *rue intérieure* undulating across several levels and connecting all functions into one continuous circuit, completed by an external segment of public and semipublic roof terraces. Typologically the range of apartments is extremely wide: Kalkbreite provides 97 dwelling units organized into 55 apartments, varying from studios and live-work units to large flat shares of up to fifteen inhabitants, and three cluster apartments of ten units each. Kraftwerk 1 and Kalkbreite convey the complexity and particularity of the co-operative scenarios. In the last years several other such developments have been completed and more still are being planned on the "rust belt" of decommissioned industry or the green periphery. Their scale and frequency have a palpable impact on the city, demonstrating a new impulse towards densification as well as other forms of environmental and social sustainability.[16]

Flagship: Mehr als Wohnen, 2007

In 2007, on the centennial anniversary of collaborations between the city and its co-operative movement, an industrial site to the north of the city became available for a flagship project. The new co-operative Mehr als Wohnen illustrates the combined expertise of some 130 co-operatives, old and new. Subject, like Kalkbreite, to a design competition organized by the city, the winning scheme for the new co-operative was a collaboration between two young architecture firms, Futurafrosch and Duplex Architekten. The design of the thirteen on-site houses was subcontracted to a collective of five practices, including the authors of the master plan.

The thirteen "houses," all between six and seven stories high, are different in appearance and flat typology. They nevertheless remain part of the same family, brought together by their dense setting, proximity, and massing in a coherent urban development. The public and commercial functions on the ground floor — from café, shop, nursery, visitor's center with assembly and exhibition rooms, and a planned care center for the elderly — act as an open market through which the public may wander freely.

Participation

Despite their differences in circumstances and approach, all these projects were delivered through the concerted efforts of informal groups of concerned citizens, some of them directly involved in the initial 1980s activism. Their associations and action groups registered as co-operatives to seek the terrain and funding for development. Thus, the new co-ops mediate between the radical values articulated in the squatters movement and the mixture of business sense and idealism that characterizes traditional co-operatives.

The new co-operatives contribute to the city both in terms of urban regeneration and gentrification, with the redevelopment of industrial districts benefiting co-operatives and the city alike. Kraftwerk 1 Hardturm started with the premise of "building the site"— creating a place where there previously was none.[17] It established connections and exchanges with existing communities, and its residential infrastructure contributed to their own urban reintegration while waiting for the city growth to catch up. Although Kalkbreite is inclusive in its social mix, as a new urban and cultural landmark it seems to contribute to Aussersihl's gentrification rather than combat it. The project Mehr als Wohnen, flagship of the city/co-operative partnership, remains demographically open, most of its inhabitants recruited after the determination of the design.

The new Zurich co-operatives can be seen as the product of a "radical intelligentsia" rooted in the middle class and higher education of the 1968 and 1980 generations. While open to the interested public, the participative process and resulting brief are guided by professional members. Often architects and other consultants act on behalf of the client in the selection of the actual designers. With inevitable variations, participative processes follow a similar pattern.[18] Politically active local associations advocating the preservation or redevelopment of specific sites register as co-operatives in order to see them through. Where common land is concerned, they have to bid for the site and gain the nomination of the city. Those associations still lacking a public profile circulate their aims by advertisements, posters, and pamphlets, among other methods, to raise awareness and attract interested individuals. Due to the length of the process these are not immediately considered future residents, although some move in upon completion. Thematic interest groups are organized to deal with specific aspects of each project (program, social mix, dwelling distribution, sustainability, communal services, neighborhood interface, etc.) and their findings circulated to a central committee, alongside the input of professional consultants. The results form the basis of project documentation, which then becomes the building brief.

The Agency of Design

Although not a legal prerequisite, architectural competitions have been the default mode of commissioning co-operative housing on public (city-owned) sites. The municipality is represented on the competition panel, alongside co-operative members, specialized consultants, and various interested parties. Once the scheme has been selected, however, architects act as independent agents, developing the scheme in dialogue with focus groups and public information sessions. However, design decisions about the project's materiality, color, expression, and massing are emphatically architect-driven and not open for negotiations during the consultation processes.

Consequently, there is no recognizable stylistic preference in recent co-operative housing. The architects' creative freedom ensures variety but also an architecture that is virtually impossible to distinguish from conventional development, which is usually of a high quality. One mark of distinction is the co-operatives' acceptance of riskier approaches: experimental apartment types, sustainable building technologies, the use of unlikely locations overlooked by the housing market. The discerning eye can identify co-operatives by some external clues, in architecture as much as inhabitation: a penchant for communal external spaces and connective elements, mixed use, small businesses, street art, gardening allotments, solar panels, and ample bicycle parking.

Architecturally, the most innovative aspect of the recent co-operative developments is internal: it consists of in-house communal facilities and new apartment types, emphasizing forms of communal living alternative to the family model. Taking their cue from the high number of one- and two-person households on the market, co-operatives experiment with larger flats in which smaller private units (bedrooms of studios) are provided. Starting from where traditional co-operatives left off, these dwelling types deconstruct the Fordist model of rooms with predetermined or fixed functions to provide ambiguous configurations that are "less defined spatial systems, testing the traditional borders of privacy." [19] Presumably, the more co-operative housing is built along these lines, the more the new typologies will consolidate and consultation processes will find it harder to come up with new insights. As briefing documents become more streamlined, architects are increasingly aware in advance of the requirements and possibilities specific to co-operative projects, their economic and ecological issues.[20] There has been a spike in publications celebrating virtually each new project with a wealth of research, statistics, and technical information. In other words, co-operative living is once more a *brand*. Historically established co-operatives are inevitably informed and become animated by the same strategies in the current quest for densification. It is only a matter of time before the new forms of collective living are popularized, adopted, and widely appropriated by the market — a revolution by stealth.

Architectural Iconography

A transition is perceptible between the intuitive improvisation of the first Kraftwerk 1 development to formalized processes involving thematic interest groups, co-operative representatives, and official partners such as the city or investors. In turn, architects are increasingly savvy about the specific design requirements of radical co-ops, leading to a more precise competition pitch and higher degrees of experimentation. Despite the variety of sizes and configurations, the new co-operative schemes adhere to a set of distinguishing features.

Mixed residential, communal, and commercial use: Kalkbreite's declared aim to create a "piece of the city" implies the idea of dense, instantly lively, porous communities, deliberately contrasting both the perimeter block colony and the isolated suburban *Siedlung*. The extent and nature of communal facilities varies from case to case: Kraftwerk 1 features a communal laundry, canteen, organic produce shop, and community hall, while Kalkbreite boasts the addition of a circular internal route, a hotel, and small rooms bookable for individual use. All of them offer on-site childcare, and Mehr als Wohnen has allowed for an old-age care facility in the future.

All use a wide range of flat types, from conventional nuclear family apartments to experimental types of communal and cluster apartments for small collectives of singles and couples, including the elderly. The efficient use of space is a paramount preoccupation: the surface per capita is smaller than on the market and regulated in co-operative statutes. The typological variety is based on the premise that co-op members will change flats as their life circumstances change.

Social mix: In partnership with the city and specialized foundations, a percentage of apartments are set aside as public housing for large families, immigrants, disabled people, etc. Special care is given to avoiding stigmatization by making subsidized flats inconspicuous. While aiming to reflect the population mix by using the city statistics as a marker, most co-operative inhabitants are Swiss or German speakers, professional and middle class.

Ecology: You can clearly point out a radical co-op by the amount of photovoltaic units on its roof. Constructions comply with Minergie ecology standards. Residents are dissuaded from wasting energy in everyday household tasks and sometimes asked to relinquish private cars. Connected to the environmentalist aspects of the earlier squats, these ecological concerns represent another instance of the institutionalization of a grassroots ethos. The squatters' militant environmentalism has been translated into official policy (The 2000-Watt Society), building standards (Minergie), and public display as *Kunst am Bau* (Badenerstrasse). Interestingly, the imposition of a lifestyle has been perceived as an imposition on individual freedom, highlighting that co-operative life comes with communal duties, and remains a matter of personal choice.

Connectivity: The architecture of radical co-operatives is awash with bridges, interior streets, and shared terraces. A somewhat literal indicator of communitarian life, the expression of physical connections between buildings is a feature borrowed from the improvised connections between occupied buildings. At the Stauffacher and subsequent squats, balconies and roof terraces played a demonstrative role as places for social exchange and production. In the new co-ops, the use of the *Dachterrasse* (roof terraces) for communal activities and energy collection retains this didactic aspect, distinguishing them from conventional houses where private terraces are less used and subject to neighborly negotiation. The creation of connections and permeable interfaces, inhabited facades, and intensely used roofs represents an iconographical marker for radical co-op ideology.

Autonomy: Programmatically, radical co-ops imply autonomy through their closed ecosystems of organic food culture, supply, and preparation. This autonomy is also conveyed as a spatial configuration. In adapting the conventional solution of the perimeter block, Kalkbreite quotes an urban configuration whose ubiquity and pragmatism achieves consistent street frontages and a feeling of urban density. At the same time it continues a long tradition of autonomous enclosures designating utopian typologies. Following from the industrial colonies of 1920s Zurich and bolo configurations, the new co-operatives are inscribed into an ambivalent urban order that conveys both autonomy and integration.

Conclusion

The agency of design plays an ambiguous role in Zurich's co-operative phenomenon. In new co-operatives, architects are involved on both sides of the commissioning process: on the one hand as clients that identify sites with potential, explore new planning possibilities, and advise development committees; on the other as external experts, professionally competing to interpret the results of the consultation process as concrete designs with autonomous artistic ambitions. Thus, architecture mediates between a collectivist ideology radical in origins, experimentation with new spatial systems and living patterns, and an external image virtually indistinguishable from that of the ever-expanding and densifying city. That said, the architecture of Zurich's new co-operatives is not nearly as radical as the ideology underlining it. Its complex configurations are shaped both by public consultation and sinuous alliances with local authorities and commercial partners. The co-operative phenomenon is tied to Zurich's transition to global city, and remains consistent — despite marked efforts to the contrary — with the gentrification and urban upgrade associated with this status.[21] The co-operative model has proven an effective tool for translating the social idealism of squat activism into concrete economic proposals, recreating the bolo as a viable business entity. The binary opposition of squatters versus establishment has converged with the historical partnership of co-operatives with the city, with the common aim of housing for all. Born from resistance to capitalism, the negotiated utopia of co-operatives is itself governed by principles of economy.

An earlier version of this paper was presented at the session "Housing and the Grassroots" at the 3rd EAHN Conference in Dublin (June 2016). The research was conducted at ETH Zurich through a postdoctoral grant offered by the SNSF Marie Heim Vögtlin Program. The author would like to thank Andreas Hofer (Kraftwerk 1) for generously sharing information and research material.

1 See René Roca, "The Cooperative Principle as the Basis of Swiss Political Culture: Past and Present," **Current Concerns** no. 11 (March 12, 2012): 10–13.
2 Walter Ruf, **Das gemeinnützige Baugenossenschaftswesen der Schweiz** (Zurich: Neuland Verlag, 1930), 21.
3 See Dominique Boudet, ed., **New Housing in Zurich: Typologies for a Changing Society** (Zurich: Park Books, 2017).
4 For a brief history of Zurich collective housing, see Daniel Kurz, "Die Genossenschaft baut mit an einer besseren Menschengemeinschaft: Wurzeln und Entwicklungslinien des gemeinnützigen Wohnens," www.wbg-zh.ch (website), 2012, 9–21, http://www.wbg-h.ch/wp-content/uploads/2012/04/Geschichte-des-genossenschaftlichen-Wohnungsbaus-in-Z%C3%BCrich.pdf.
5 Ibid., 10.
6 For a more detailed survey of the reform movement refer to Kurz, "Lebensreform und Gartenstadt," in **Die Disziplinierung der Stadt: Moderner Städtebau in Zürich, 1900 bis 1940** (Zurich: gta Verlag, 2008), 115–18.
7 Alison Ravetz, **Council Housing and Culture: The History of a Social Experiment** (London: Routledge, 2001), 5.
8 In the last two decades, the decommissioning of industrial areas, especially along the railway (Zurich West, Oerlikon, etc.) has provided ample opportunities for the new construction. Prior to being redeveloped, several dormant postindustrial sites were occupied by squatters and became temporary centers of alternative culture (Wohlgroth Areal, 1991–1993, Kalkbreite, 2003–2008, Binz Areal, 2006–2013).
9 P.M., **bolo'bolo** (Zurich: Paranoia Citz, 1983). All following quotes are from the English thirtieth-anniversary edition (Brooklyn: Autonomia/Ardent, 2011), 23.
10 Ibid., 86–87.
11 Ibid., 68.
12 "Introduction to Second English Edition, Apology – A Decade Later" (1993), in ibid., 23.
13 Martin Blum, Andreas Hofer, and P. M., **KraftWerk 1: Projekt für das Sulzer-Escher Wyss Areal** (Zurich: Paranoia City, 1993).
14 See **Tec21**, no. 42 (2001).
15 See Andreas Hofer, "Von der Familienwohnung zum Cluster-Grundriss," **Tec21** 137, no. 7 (2011): 23–31.
16 See Dominique Boudet, "Zurich: More Than Housing," in **More Than Housing: Cooperative Planning – A Case Study in Zurich** (Basel: Birkhäuser, 2015), 17.
17 Andreas Hofer, interviewed by the author, Zurich, April 2016.
18 See Margrit Hugentobler, "Discussion: Participation Generates Identification," in **More Than Housing: Co-operative Planning, a Case Study in Zurich** (Basel: Birkhäuser, 2015), 105–10.
19 Andreas Hofer interview, 2016.
20 Ibid.
21 See also Irina Davidovici, "3/5 - Zürich: Zurigo, Zu Reich," **Casabella** 861 (2016): 77–79.

Freedom to Co-operate: Urban Informality and Micro-political Counterrevolutions in Brazil

Rainer Hehl

Despite changing political constellations, one phenomenon stands out as a constant factor overlooking the housing production in Brazil over the past 120 years. The ongoing rise of urban informality and the spread of self-built settlements since the beginning of the twentieth century stems from the lacking capacity to formally provide housing solutions for the growing urban population—but it also reflects city's bottom-up organization by its inhabitants. Even though the so-called favelas are mainly associated with poverty and marginality, they play a significant role within local economies and form the very basis for the self-governed city constituted by community associations and local networks that are managing these neighborhoods either independently or in coordination with municipal institutions. Favelas bear the potential to be operated through co-operative models as well as being breeding grounds for micro-political mobilization from below. However, the history of urban informality in Brazil shows that efforts to turn these places into democratically operated communities largely failed. What is needed to organize the informal in ways that would allow the inhabitants to take control of their own livelihoods and transform themselves into self-organized neighborhoods committed to good urban governance?

The evolution of the favelas in Brazil can be seen as a constant micro-political force that underwent various manifestations and organizational forms ranging from community-based action to parallel systems organized by criminal fractions and entangled with official politics. Looking backwards, the turbulent history of the informal city in Brazil was marked by various moments of transformation, not only concerning the relationship between the formal and the informal, but also in terms of the production of subjectivities and the formation of a collective consciousness. These transformations have to be seen in the context of changing economic and political regimes, which along different stages gradually gained control over informal settlements by directly or indirectly instrumentalizing urban informality for their own benefit. Informality thus became a micro-political tool for an emerging neoliberal market economy and therefore played a significant role in consolidating political and economic power constellations.[1] As the impact of this influence was directly affecting the constitution of bottom-up actors, it also determined the way self-organization was played out and perceived. Instead of gaining autonomy, micro-political movements on the ground were gradually incorporated into a system in which the boundaries between formal and informal, between legal and illegal, between state authority and criminal activity are blurred. What is more, the intertwining between macro- and micro-political actors eventually led to the subjection of self-organizing entities to repressive regimes. In turn, liberation from these regimes can only stem from a project of a micro-political counterrevolution, which reestablishes the preconditions for civic engagement and awareness for the city as collective project. As it will be shown in the following argumentation, counterinsurgency against recent attempts to destabilize democratic institutions can only be successful if it is focused on the production of multiple subjectivities who are collectively managing the urban commons and shared resources.

A Brief History of Urban Informality in Brazil

The emergence of the favelas is historically marked by the abolishment of slavery in 1888, and more precisely by the end of the Canudos War (1895–96), when government soldiers who were defeating secessionist insurrections in the northeast of Brazil returned to Rio de Janeiro and, lacking adequate shelter, started to squat on the hills in the center of the city.[2] The name “favela” refers to a plant that is found in arid zones of Brazil and stands for resistance—the favelas were initially established as a form of protest against the inability of the local government to resolve the housing question.

As this question remained unresolved over the course of the following decades, favelas grew consistently, amounting to 7 percent of the urban population of Rio de Janeiro in the 1950s.[3] Given the rising scope of informal settlement, by then they couldn’t be neglected anymore. The favelas turned from blind spots on the map to strategically important areas for electoral campaigns. Clientelism and co-optation started to be recurrent practices for breaking deals with informal communities and getting their votes in return. In order to avoid these communities gaining too much autonomy over their self-governed territories, politicians had to "climb up, before communists will climb down the hills" and have an influence on official politics — a slogan that represents an early attempt to demonize self-organization as Marxist plot.[4] But in the beginning of the 1960s favelas were finally discovered as assets for a growing real estate market and, in the wake of their relocation, for a growing construction sector. Located on valuable sites in central areas, favelas promised to generate profits if their inhabitants were to be evicted and the land liberated for real estate speculation

Furthermore, with the removal of the favela dwellers to the urban periphery an expanding market for mass housing was created. The settlements that were established in the 1960s — Villa Kennedy, Villa Aliança, and Cidade de Deus — were developed as exemplary cases for a new paradigm in urban development. Sponsored by US authorities and promoted through the program Alliance for Progress, these relocation projects sought to turn the poor populations into homeowners and middle-class consumers for the capitalist market

Despite the fact that this strategy was persistently pushed by the upcoming military regime, favelas continued to grow in the following decades. What is more, the newly established units were informalized and turned into favelas shortly after their erection, as the case of Cidade de Deus vividly shows.[5] Urban informality persisted as a layer of self-organization beyond state control, and, as the case of Cidade de Deus also illustrates, as a parallel world increasingly dominated by criminal factions. In retrospect, the favela interventions during the military regime turned out to be twofold.

While evictions and relocations served to fuel the engine of real estate development and large-scale construction companies, the growing number of favelas also became the target for another kind of mafia — the so-called milicia. At the end of the 1960s, militias emerged as extermination groups composed of military police officers and other agents from security forces that acted as for-hire assassins. These death squads arrived in full force in the 1970s.

After a while, civilians began to emerge as the leaders of these paramilitary groups — but they were always tied to government agents. Since then, the militias have formed the direct link between the political regime and criminal organizations controlling the favelas. Instead of focusing on drug trafficking, the militia network is set up as a power structure based on the collection of fees on properties and businesses in return for "security services."[6] In other words, the militia is focused on the extraction of profits from the informal economy, a sector that grew significantly starting in the 1970s.

The fact that formal and informal structures are highly entangled became ever more obvious with the installment of neoliberal policies during the 1970s, and it turned out to be a predominant factor for the mushrooming of the favelas in the 1980s and 1990s when the highest growth rates were registered. The correlation between the neoliberal economy and favela growth mainly stems from the fact that informality provided low-wage labor necessary to guarantee the extraction of surplus value. This also explains why the informal city is still growing at the same speed as the formal housing market, or even exceeding it.

During the democratization process after the end of the military regime, reformist forces finally recognized the self-organizing capacity of informal settlements and promoted favela upgrading, mainly through the improvement of infrastructure services and community facilities. Projects were undertaken by keeping the existing social structure in place while introducing participatory forms of development. Despite the apparent success of these programs in providing basic services and fostering community-led development, the dichotomy between formal and informal still dominates the housing question. This is why the same patterns (eviction, relocation, control by parallel organizations, etc.) still seem to determine favela politics. However a current shift in the macro-political constellation is now having an increasing effect on micro-political organization on the ground and fundamentally changing the way in which bottom-up organizations are instrumentalized by the neoliberal market economy.

When, in the early 1980s, Brazil returned to democracy after two decades of military dictatorship, the country was filled with hope and expectations. It was the moment when various social movements and associations gathered for a debate aimed at the revitalization of political institutions and the elaboration of a new constitution. For the French psychoanalyst Felix Guattari and his Brazilian colleague Suely Rolnik, this revitalization process did not only concern the social and political conscious of the Brazilian society but also the country's unconscious. In 1982, they undertook an extensive trip around Brazil in order to participate in a series of talks, roundtable discussions, meetings, and encounters with groups and movements in order to document the status quo of a country in transformation. It was particularly important for this project to record the voices of marginalized population groups, activists for the homeless and for gay rights, and representatives of the workers unions in order to get a complete picture of the "strategies of desires in the social field," for which Guattari and Rolnik coined the term "micro-politics."[7] This moment of micro-political transformation gave rise to optimism, later described by Guattari in the subsequent publication *Molecular Revolution in Brazil* as "a period of productivity, proliferation, creation, utterly fabulous revolutions from the viewpoint of the emergence of a people." The revolutions that were happening at that moment were taking place on a "molecular" level, as they were directly affecting desires, subjectivity, and the relationship with the other. According to Guattari and Rolnik, the task from then on would be to trace new cartographies of collective interaction that would enable the undoing of centuries of regimes of exclusion (colonial, slave-holding, dictatorial, and capitalist) and to reconfigure social hierarchies. What is particularly instructive in this attempt to construct new outlines of reality is revealing the role of the production of subjectivity in the process of micro-political mobilization. As Guattari claims, "The emergence of a multiple people cannot be reduced to the formation of identities stemming from language, the family and social relations, but rather has to include all productive forces shaping subjectivities." Under the reign of capitalism, which Guattari called "Integrated World Capitalism" (IWC), subjectivity is not just situated in the individual field but in every process of social and material production. The production of subjectivity in IWC "does not consist solely of the production of power to control social and productive relations. The production of subjectivity is the raw material for any and all production."[8] Emphasizing modes of subjectivation, the revolution at that time was about mobilizing productive forces that would lead to a reconfiguration of representation, behavior, sensibility, perception, memory, social and sexual relations, imaginaries, etc.

Despite the fact that the democratization process also led to the rise of the Workers' Party (PT) under former union leader Luiz Inácio Lula de Silva and its election victory for the federal government in 2003, it seems that the expectations for social change were gradually eroded by another kind of micro-revolution, which eventually led in 2016 to the takeover by reactionary forces joining two seemingly opposed political strategies — a radical commitment to the neoliberal market economy and the advancement of a repressive fascist regime backed by the military.

What happened in the meantime that led to a fallback of a macro-political setup, which bears an uncanny resemblance to conditions during Brazil's military regimes?

Guattari and Rolnik pointed out that neoliberal capitalist production mainly operates through a very specific kind of production of subjectivity, which is individualized, standardized, and centralized around an image or identity. What makes it so hard to recognize the normative power of neoliberal modes of subjectivation is related to the illusion that neoliberalism is built up on the promise of freedom, understood as the freedom of individuals to be part of a market system of free exchange of goods and commodities. But what if a majority of the population is excluded from this type of market system?

The disillusionment that was experienced by a large segment of a newly emerging middle class after a decade of socialist-democratic government mainly stemmed from the mismatch between rising expectations during a period of economic growth and a harsh reality that didn't allow the majority to partake in capitalist value creation. Despite tremendous efforts to redistribute national revenue via state-sponsored programs (Bolsa Familia, Minha Casa Minha Vida), the social agenda of a left-wing government wasn't able to cope with the dominating logic of market interests.

The masses of protestors filling the streets in 2013 who aimed for better urban services, health care, and education represented the largest demonstrations Brazil had ever seen. However, it didn't trigger a radical change of the causes of unequal distribution and poor urban management: an urban economy based on speculative profits backed up by a financial regime defending corporate against public interests.[9]

It is ironic that the protests culminated in the impeachment of the socialist-democratic president in 2016 and in the installment of a political regime that has since systematically dismantled democratic institutions and social policies. With the election of a far-right president in 2018, it became clear that the revolution Guattari and Rolnik were anticipating in the 1980s failed. Instead, another micro-political transformation was pushed forward, driven by reactionary and neoliberal forces at the same time. The political actions that have taken place since the takeover of power demonstrate that the normative settings of neoliberal politics are not necessarily contradictory to fascist indoctrination. The micro-political dimension of the current phase of the seizure of economic, political, and social power becomes evident in its direct influence on the production of subjectivity. The policies that have been implemented since then are obviously directed against any kind of emergence of a multiple people as it was described by Guattari and Rolnik. With the dismantling of the educational system and its alignment with far-right ideologies — the quasi-abolishment of social programs, the oppression of non-governmental organizations, the persecution of human-rights activists and political opponents, the marginalization of the poor and black population, and the stigmatization of social movements as Marxist conspirators — the current government in Brazil is directly attacking any kind of emergence of multiple subjectivities. Or, in the words of Suely Rolnik, "While (in the wake of the second phase of the coup d'état) the macro-political operation of dismantling the Constitution and the national economy is intensifying, the micro-political operation of production of subjectivities by manipulating the desires of the people is also intensifying. With the double-fold operation of two facets that cannot be dissociated, another third and ultimate phase of the coup d'état is about to be prepared: the complete takeover of political and economic power by globalized capitalism."[10]

What would be needed now to overthrow the current power system is a new kind of micro-political counterrevolution.

Rio das Pedras

The fact that the growth of the favelas nowadays is in parallel or is even outpacing formal developments is most visible in Rio das Pedras, one of Rio de Janeiro's largest favelas, located in the western part of the metropolitan region. Because of its proximity to Barra da Tijuca, the cities' major expansion zone for real estate development, Rio das Pedras emerged in the 1970s as a suburban neighborhood providing informal housing for the increased demand for labor in the area. Due to its defined borders and its vital local economy, the neighborhood can be considered a city within the city, which created its own distinct identity through informal construction and self-organization. Composed predominantly of urban migrants from the northeastern region of Brazil, Rio das Pedras developed over the last two decades into an important hub for local trade boosting commercial activities and contributing to the ongoing growth of its population, which counts today officially about 60,000 inhabitants. The community association has its own chamber of commerce overseeing the activities of local shop owners, services, and transport co-operatives guaranteeing rapid connection to the rest of the city.[11] The strength of its local economy, which accounts for 40 percent of the inhabitants' revenues, is partially owed to the presence of the militia, which controls building activities, collects fees (extortions), and "takes care" of the security of the residents. Rio das Pedras was even declared the headquarters of one of the largest militia organizations — its entanglement with the military, the civil police, and politicians from the municipal government was also the subject of the movie *Tropa de Elite II* (Elite Squad), directed by José Padilha, which revealed the scope of criminal activities of a network of corrupt politicians, former policemen, firefighters, and security agents who were controlling, seizing, and legalizing land ownership — sometimes even through the city by paying property taxes. As the land system is not properly regulated, the militia members take hold of informal areas and then start to sell them. While illegal land occupations were initially the target of the militias, their core activity is expanding: besides the collection of fees they are also selling basic services and urban commodities such as water and land.

The case of Rio das Pedras attracted particular attention as the death squad of the militia, popularly known under the name *escritório do crime* (Crime Bureau), has been involved in the murder of Rio city councillor Marielle Franco, who was executed on the street in March 2018. A local black activist, Marielle Franco grew up in a favela and defended the cause of favela residents against the growing influence of the milicia and its violent strategies. As a woman of color and favela resident who also made her gay relationship public, Franco represented all aspects of marginalized populations — and her death became exemplary for the brutality of current power relations and gave her the status of an icon for the fight against oppression. The investigation of the plot leading to her assassination made no progress until it was handed over to the federal police, who uncovered the aforementioned link to the militia, resulting in the arrest of two suspects in March 2019, one year after the assassination took place. Almost simultaneously, another link between militia and politicians was revealed. The son of the acting president, who is deputy in the Rio de Janeiro state legislative assembly, employed the head of the Crime Bureau (Adriano Magalhães de Nóbrega) in his cabinet. He is also involved in a corruption scheme, which draws evens wider circles of a network between the militia and family members.[12] While the investigation is ongoing, the connection between an intricate network of criminal action taking control of the favelas and its informal economy and official state power of the highest level became obvious.

The case of Rio das Pedras is exemplary as it illustrates bluntly the entanglement between macro-politics and micro-political constellations. But it also demonstrates the extent to which the control over the informal correlates with the control over the production of subjectivities. Marielle Franco, representing the voice of the favelados and defending the rights of the many, became the target of the regime precisely because she stands for the emergence of a multiple people. While historically clientelism and co-optation were widespread means to instrumentalize favela residents for political goals, the interference is now reaching other dimensions. In a situation were "the militia is the government," the rules of the game are determined according to the law of the strongest. The manipulation of official media in order to obscure criminal relationships between micro- and macro-levels further contributes to the suspension of formal frameworks that would guarantee a legal dialogue between bottom-up organization and top-down state institutions.

While complex relationships between politicians, militias, and residents increasingly contribute to the proliferation of a mafia state, Rio das Pedras continues to grow. Rather than asking what the future of the informal will be, the question is to what extent self-organization can still be based on democratic models and escape the perfidious strategies of suppressive regimes. Considering the fact that these regimes operate within the paradigm of a neoliberal market economy based on private interests and the dismantling of regulating state institutions, an alternative take on the political economy is needed. The new deal for this economy can only be formulated on the micro-political level — the more we direct our attention to the production of multiple subjectivities who co-operate and collectively manage the urban commons, the more resistance is built up to counteract the takeover by an alliance between criminal factions, neoliberal agents, and reactionary forces.

How to form a group of people who are committed to share living space and resources was a major concern for the municipal government of São Paulo in the beginning of the 1990s. Under the government of Mayor Luiza Erundina, housing projects were launched for co-operative developments based on the model of the Mutirão — self-managed construction co-ops that significantly improved the standards and variety for low-income housing. Within a time frame of three years, these experiments led to the emergence of NGOs and architecture offices specialized in social and technical assistance for self-organizing entities. The experiments in co-operative developments have to be seen in the context of the democratization process and the formation of networks as described in Guattari and Rolnik's investigation on the "molecular revolution in Brazil." The micro-political mobilization taking place at that time in Brazil was not only limited to the reestablishment of political institutions but comprised a larger educational project of knowledge transfer that sought to bring diverse actors together and strengthen civic consciousness and engagement. What has been termed "technical assistance" included the transfer of skills and knowledge to communities in order to empower them to take care of their proper concerns, from administrative and budgetary management to project development and the supervision of complex construction processes. Capacity building was understood as a collective effort that required the distribution of roles and responsibilities within the formation of a common ground that can be shared by all of the members. The Mutirão as a model of mutual self-help was therefore extended into a nucleus for democratic processes. The production of subjectivities that would enable the formation of democracy from below was orchestrated through regularly scheduled community meetings and physically expressed through assembly spaces that were particularly designed to represent commitment to communality and joint action.

The knowledge that has been gathered with this experience played an important role in the implementation of co-operative models thirty years later within the framework of the state-led social housing program Minha Casa Minha Vida. The challenge of managing a self-organized co-operative housing development within the framework of a top-down governmental program tailored to the needs of the construction industries relied on social and technical assistance. The transfer of knowledge for self-organizing entities was therefore particularly difficult in remote regions where municipal governments do not dispose the know-how required to assist co-ops in the process.

How far knowledge transfer involves the production of subjectivity can be illustrated with the case of an exemplary project that has been set up in Prarauapebas, a mining town in the northern state of Para on the edge of the Amazon forest, which ranks among the fastest growing cities in Brazil.[13] Due to uncontrolled urban expansion and soaring land prices, a large number of inhabitants are housed without sufficient infrastructure in favela-like conditions. The model project was based on participatory development, with the ambition to set up a housing co-op that would provide apartments for up to 500 families. With the help of the Rio de Janeiro–based NGO Fundação Bento Rubião and local charitable institutions, the formation of the co-operative was conducted in collective sessions in which future residents set up the constellation of the housing blocks and became co-designers themselves. What was particularly difficult to accept for former favela dwellers was the fact that they would have to give up the idea of living in a single-family house. Both housing models — the informal dwelling in the favela as well as the repetitive schemes of the Minha Casa Minha Vida program — are predominantly based on privatized units. In order to change the imagination from an individualized housing model to a collective understanding of livelihood, the fundamental relationship between the intimacy of the private home and the collective realm had to be questioned. The shift from an individualized to a collective sense or subjectivity required an understanding that they would take advantage of shared facilities, and that, in the end, the whole is more than the sum of its parts. The anticipation of a future neighbor who doesn't necessarily share the same ideas had to be based upon a learning process that did not simply imply the negotiation of private interests in order to find a common denominator, but rather relied on the insight that sharing and cooperation will lead to greater affordability, flexibility, and freedom.

As the domination of individualized subjectivity can be considered the driving force of a neoliberal market system based on surplus value and privatized profits, co-op subjectivity provides the prerequisite for a counter-model to current modes of housing production.[14] The formation of knowledge and expertise for participatory developments, the education of urban dwellers as responsible and self-managing citizens, and the increase of awareness for the urban commons represent the very basic pillars for sustainable and equitable housing development. It is no coincidence that the current government in Brazil is deliberately and strategically dismantling precisely these pillars by cutting sponsorships for NGOs, by stigmatizing any kind of mobilization for self-organization as leftist conspiracy, and by deregulating the educational system. Rebellion against privatization and commodified urban production therefore has to start with the production of subjectivities apt to conceive and develop life in common. This would be of particular importance in view of the future rise of urban informality and the prospect of mafia-like power regimes taking control of the informal city. In order to do so, the micro-political counterrevolution has to be built upon nongovernmental structures and the mobilization for joint action beyond ideological camps. Cooperation has to be established as a fundamental right extending the general claim for the right to the city, which mainly implies the dissemination of knowledge and the creation of spaces where this knowledge can be shared and applied.[15] If co-operative practice wants to become operational for a micro-political counterrevolution, it has to invest in the production of subjectivities that allow the emergence of a multiple people.

In one of his books, the British architect John Turner, who thoroughly investigated the conditions of urban informality in South America in the 1950s and 1960s, demonstrates that autonomy in building practice, where dwellers have more control over the housing process, leads to better results than top-down state-developed housing provision. The title of the book, *Freedom to Build*, evokes the importance of freedom in this process, understood as people's freedom to make key decisions by themselves. However, what wasn't properly answered at that time was the question of how freedom to make these decisions can be created. In a more recent statement, Turner explains that freedom cannot be reduced to free choices within predefined limits, but rather should enable one "to make use of one's own knowledge and skills, to do what one is able and willing to do for oneself, family, neighbours, even life as a whole. Without sufficient freedom of that real kind, in some areas of life at least, one cannot be fulfilled as a person. This is the nub of the argument: personal and locally particular activities, like housing, are potential vehicles for growth, not just things we need. So the greatest evils are actions and tools that frustrate people's abilities and will to do things in and for themselves and their own communities. You must be free to find your own way within limits that don't hurt other people or the environment, and are not counterproductive in some other way."[16] Following this interpretation, it might be better to turn the focus to the production of free-minded subjectivities who will defend our right for "freedom to co-operate."

1 The correlation between formal and informal development was the subject of the author's PhD dissertation, "Organizing the Informal: Formation and Transformation of the Informal City with Case Studies in Rio de Janeiro" (2011).

2 See "On the Origin of 'Favela,'" **RioOnWatch**, February 14, 2012, https://www.rioonwatch.org/?p=2920.

3 Currently the percentage of informal settlements in Rio de Janeiro amounts to about 24 percent. See Censos Demográficos, IBGE Rio de Janeiro, 2018.

4 Quote from L. P. Valladares, **Passa-se uma Casa: Análise do Programa da Remoção de Favelas do Rio de Janeiro** (Rio de Janeiro: Jorge Zahar Editor, 1978).

5 The case of Cidade de Deus is the subject of M. Angélil and R. Hehl, **Cidade de Deus: Working with Informalized Mass Housing in Brazil** (Berlin: Ruby Press, 2013).

6 See "In Rio de Janeiro, the Militia Isn't a Parallel Power. It's the Government.," **RioOnWatch**, March 12, 2019, https://www.rioonwatch.org/?p=51031.

7 See F. Guattari and S. Rolnik, **Molecular Revolution in Brazil** (Los Angeles: Semiotext(e), 2007).

8 Ibid.

9 The ascent of real estate and construction companies gradually dominating urban development in Brazil is clearly illustrated in what Raquel Rolnik terms the Real-Estate-Financial Complex. R. Rolnik, **Urban Warfare: Housing Under the Empire of Finance** (London: Verso, 2019), 201–64.

10 S. Rolnick, "O seriado do golpe em três temporadas," **Outras Palavras**, February 4, 2018, https://outraspalavras.net/sem-categoria/666381/. Quote translated by the author.

11 See "Rio das Pedras: An Overview of the Bustling West Zone Favela," **RioOnWatch**, September 13, 2016, https://www.rioonwatch.org/?p=30692.

12 In addition to obvious links between the militia and the president's family, it was revealed during the investigation that one of the suspects for Marielle Franco's assassination was living in the same condominium complex as the president, and the other suspect proudly published a selfie with the president on his Facebook account.

13 A detailed description of the urban growth in Parauapebas can be found in R. Hehl, "Natural City Parauapebas: Frontier Town of Global Capitalism," in **Empower! Essays on the Political Economy of Urban Form**, vol. 3, ed. M. Angélil and R. Hehl (Berlin, Ruby Press, 2014).

14 Raquel Rolnik describes how individual private property became hegemonic over the course the last 250 years of the social relationship between humanity and territory. She also demonstrates how the liberal conception of freedom ultimately depends on the guarantee of private property. See Rolnik, **Urban Warfare**, 150.

15 David Harvey describes in his text "The Right to the City" how the production of subjectivity plays a crucial role in the collective project of city making: "The right to the city is far more than a right of individual access to the resources that the city embodies: it is a right to change ourselves by changing the city more after our heart's desire. It is, moreover, a collective rather than an individual right since changing the city inevitably depends upon the exercise of a collective power over the processes of urbanization. The freedom to make and remake ourselves and our cities is, I want to argue, one of the most precious yet most neglected of our human rights." D. Harvey, "The Right to the City," **New Left Review**, no. 53 (September–October 2008), https://newleftreview.org/issues/II53/articles/david-harvey-the-right-to-the-city.

16 John. F. C Turner, interview by Roberto Chavez with Julie Viloria and Melanie Zipperer, World Bank, September 11, 2000, siteresources.worldbank.org/INTUSU/Resources/turner-tacit.pdf.

Donas da Terra: Women Role Models in Social Leadership

Paula Constante &
Patricia Ventura

In an attempt to intuit the profound and sensitive nature of micropolitical processes, these images trace short biographies of female actors who took charge of their own personal transformation, thereby initiating a deeply instinctive change in their communities. Strong female social leaders were micro-politically fighting for the right to build their homes — if necessary, with their own hands. As a result, self-transformation and emancipation occurred through bold engagement in the buildup process of sustainable homes, safe neighborhoods, and sensitive communities. The insurrection of female courage led to new gender roles and models of social leadership, capable of mobilizing and inspiring entire communities and future generations. Micro-political transformation focuses on the collective occupation of territories, be they spatial, physical, psychological, linguistic, social, political, or cultural, in order to achieve peripheral integration and empowerment through authentic democratic interactions. The living examples of thousands of women engaged in the re-territorialization of subjectivities bear perceptive witness to this multilayered, micro-political transformation of territories. Their faces, stories, and words stand for the struggles, resistance, and victories that indeed allowed them to become *donas da terra* — "female holders of the earth."

Oppressed people hardly ever get to write their own story. Even if they try, there must be a constant effort to gather, organize, and compile images, texts, and documents. And not only that: a story must be told to *somebody*, otherwise it will never exist. Those who struggle on a daily basis can barely find the energy to take care of what has already happened, let alone document it.

The Movimento Sem Terra Leste 1 (Landless Movement of East Zone 1) is a Brazilian popular housing movement that constructs homes using mutual-help efforts and self-management in the East Zone of São Paulo. The movement reached its thirtieth anniversary in 2017. To celebrate, its organizers invited the architect and documentarist Paula

Constante to research, compile, and narrate their stories from the movement's inception to today.

The research work has been developed since 2015, with the organization of imagery, newspapers and documents, and also video footage of demonstrations, interviews and all kinds of gatherings and activities promoted by the movement. The idea is to narrate this huge effort to build collective and self-managed urban habitats.

The portraits and quotes presented here are extracted from some of the video interviews captured from women social leaders of different periods of the movement's history. All of them still are connected to the movement today. These excerpts, combined with the stories of the thousands of other people who make up the movement, aim to give voice to the activists who form the basis for micro-political change.[1]

Evaniza Rodriguez

Evaniza joined the movement in 1988. As an almost founding member, she already followed the boom of occupations that were taking place in the 1980s when she was an engaged teenager in the youth pastoral of the Catholic Church. She chose to study social work and has been working with the movement ever since. She is fully and deeply dedicated to the movement, with a coherence and simplicity that inspire other followers.

"Cada ação que a gente faz, tem o significado de questionar a ordem social vigente. Então, a ação do movimento busca transformar o estado. Mas principalmente transformar a sociedade. Talvez mais importante que transformar o Estado seja transformar a sociedade."

Every action we make is intended to question the current social order. So, the movement's actions pursue state-level change. But mainly, we want to change society itself. Perhaps even more important than changing the state is changing society.

Cristiane Lima, Rose Queiroz, and Mariza Dutra

Cristiane joined the movement on May 10, 1997, when she was about to get married. In 1999, construction began on the co-operative housing project Paulo Freire. She and her husband were elected to be the caretakers of the project during the construction period. At that time, her husband also became project manager of the co-op project. They had a son, Matheus. Later, throughout the extended construction process, she was also elected coordinator. While shy, she radiates a profoundly generous lucidity. Cris has remained until today a grassroots social leader and project manager for Mutirãos.

Rose joined the movement in July 1998 through the Church of Good Hope. She participated in the entire process of the Mutirão movement. With two daughters, she emancipated herself from her marriage because she felt finally capable to take care of them alone; as a single mother she became after all autonomous, political, and a whole citizen and social leader of her community. Rose went to meetings with the government and with the National Housing Movement Union. She came back to tell the community in detail everything she had heard and said. She enrolled in university at the age of fifty to study social work. In every conversation, she is joyful and has an infectious smile.

Mariza joined the movement on August 5, 1998. She was paying rent in a two-room apartment to live there with her five children. Their association was from another housing co-operative right next to the co-operative Paulo Freire. The two co-operatives became joint brothers thanks to Mariza's curiosity and the connections she made. She has a unique speaking force felt by everyone when she raises her voice during demonstrations. Even with difficult scars from the past, Mariza remains resilient.

Cristiane Lima: "Nós não nos víamos como pessoas políticas dentro da sociedade. Nos víamos como mais um, como mais tantos por aí. Acho que todo mundo que entra no movimento não sai da mesma forma que entrou. Nos vemos como cidadãos políticos ativos nesses processos. E isso ninguém quer que a gente seja."

> Cristiane Lima: We did not see ourselves as political beings in our society. We used to see ourselves as just one more among so many others here. I think that nobody who got into the movement comes out of it the same person they were before. We start seeing ourselves as citizens, as politically active beings. But this is something that nobody wants us to be.

Rose Queiroz: "E o processo longo ensinou que a coordenação não foi fácil. E o conhecimento começa aí. Você vai numa

Prefeitura ouvir o movimento dialogar. O movimento é realmente uma faculdade."

> Rose Queiroz: The long Mutirão construction process has taught me that leading and coordinating are not easy. That is exactly where our knowledge begins. You go to the city hall and listen to how the movement negotiates. You learn as if you were attending college.

Mariza Dutra: "Sou coordenadora executiva financeira da União dos Movimentos de Moradia. E lá na União fazemos um projeto participativo em todas as instâncias do governo: município, estado e federação. Tem vezes que cansa, sou mãe, mulher. Mas as companheiras estão aqui sempre dando força, choro com elas, desabafo. São espelhos para mim."

> Mariza Dutra: I am the financial executive coordinator of the Housing Movement Union. There, in the union, we fight to implement participatory projects at all levels of government: municipal, state, and federal. Sometimes it is tiring — I am a mother, I am

a woman. But my companions always give me strength: they cry with me, they help me unburden. They are my own mirror.

Maria Isabel Nobre de Souza

Isabel joined the movement in mid-1989. She was looking for a greater meaning in life after a significant personal disappointment. She was studying but did not achieve a recognized diploma, because the course she attended turned out to be irregular. It was in the movement that Isabel understood very clearly the importance of critical knowledge and collective action in terms of strengthing one's power as a citizen.

Maria Isabel Nobre de Souza: "CDHU não queria aceitar esse projeto porque não era projeto para pobre com esse tamanho todo. Emperraram muito, devido nossa teimosia. Nossa área é de 64 m^2 e queriam nos dar um de 30 e poucos. Era o dobro do tamanho que o da CDHU."

Maria Isabel Nobre de Souza: The housing secretary of the state of São Paulo would not approve our architectural project. They said it was not adequate for poor people because it was too big. So they stalled us with bureaucracy. But we were stubborn. Our apartments now are 64 square meters, while the standard used to be approximately 35. Our design was twice as big as what they offered.

Lucimara Santos

Lucimara founded the Landless Movement of East Zone 1 along with Rita Angelus. She lived the dynamics of the first meetings she attended as a tenement dweller of *cortiços*, tenement houses for the poor in the center of the city. Social leadership was formed at a time when there were no past references — Brazil was still freeing itself from the dictatorship when the movement began. It was the experience of each meeting, each occupation, the moments lived in pure solidarity and creative boldness that make up the modus operandi of the entire movement to this day.

Lucimara Santos: "Não é pegar a casa. Tem que fazer a convivência com o bairro. Vira e mexe chamo reunião aí na creche. Mais eu e Conceição que estamos indo. Por isso que o movimento dá essa condição de você crescer. Não pode fazer sua casa e ficar enfiado nela. Ele é muito amplo para você crescer. Não discute só a casa, discute o bairro, a educação, a saúde, a sua convivência ..."

Lucimara Santos: It is not just about getting a house. You have to live in a community.

Every now and then, I call a meeting about our public childcare. You cannot build a house like this and shut yourself up inside of it as if nothing else was your concern. The movement teaches you that. You do not only discuss housing issues. You have to discuss the entire neighborhood and its education, health, social livelihood ...

Cristiane Dantas

Cristiane joined the movement on September 30, 2012, because her ex-boyfriend's grandmother was a *mutirant*. She was curious but still quite suspicious. Two generations later after the movement began, the situation in the country was already quite different. Cris got to know each instance of the association's political actions. Participating out of curiosity, she was suddenly "falling in love" with the movement because she understood that here she could finally help more effectively.

Cristiane Dantas: "Então isso foi assim: aonde uma moradora da Zona Leste, na periferia, sem perspectiva, jamais de ir pra Bahia com muito sacrifício ver a vó, vai chegar no Equador e representar o Brasil na parte de habitação e falar como a gente trabalha com autogestão aqui no Brasil?"

Cristiane Dantas: On what planet would a resident from São Paulo's East Zone, with no money or even prospects to be able to visit her grandmother in Bahia, now travel to Equador to represent Brazil's housing movement and show them how we work with self-management?

Zelina Pereira

Zelina joined the movement on September 25, 2011, finding out about it through a friend. She quickly began to fully participate and assume responsibilities. She always had a hard time speaking in public, and avoided any political discussions because she didn't think she understood anything correctly. She is still shy, but it doesn't stop her from speaking when needed. Today she is proud of her career and her surroundings. She understands the process and the movement as a school of life.

Zelina Pereira: "Somos referência hoje. Temos vários outros projetos para começar: Belém, São Rafael, Milton Santos. E a gente sente orgulho de quando terminar a obra aqui também poder ajudar e contribuir com nossos companheiros. E levar para eles nossa experiência, como é nossa organização."

Zelina Pereira: We are the reference today. We have several other projects that are ready to start: Belém, São Rafael, Milton Santos.

And we are proud that when we finish the work here, we can also help and contribute to all our companions. So we can bring them our experience and we can what how our organization is like.

Carol Martins

Carol joined the movement in 2014, on the recommendation of a cousin. Like many of her generation, she first needed to learn about the political potential of the co-op movement, since previously she had an immense "disbelief" in anything related to politics. But already by the time of her registration, Carol felt hope again. Through her experiences, she has recognized her strength, her power, and the capacity and possibility to dream collectively.

Carol Martins: "Hoje eu faço faculdade de Pedagogia. Foi o Movimento que trouxe esse desejo no meu coração. De querer ter conhecimento, de querer estudar."

Carol Martins: Today I'm going to college to study pedagogy. It was the movement that brought this desire into my heart: to want to have knowledge, to want to study.

Sandra Kocura

Sandra encountered the movement in 2014 as an intern for a social-technical assistance agency. One month later she applied to become a member of a housing co-op because she had no home. For her, who sees the world of social relations threatened by capitalism, the movement, which can be reflected and experienced horizontally, is a glimmer of hope.

Sandra Kocura: “Somos estigmatizados, somos ofendidos, mas somos famílias. A maioria do Movimento é de mulheres. Mulheres que são monoparentais, são as provedoras dos seus filhos e famílias. Grande parte de seu salário vai para o aluguel, vivendo nas periferias, demorando 3, 4 horas para chegar no trabalho. Isso aumenta a desigualdade.”

> Sandra Kocura: We're stigmatized, we're offended, but we're families. The majority of the movement is women. Women who are single parents are the providers of their children and families. A large part of their salary goes to rent, living in the outskirts, where it takes three, four hours to get to work. This increases inequality.

Priscila Neves

Priscila joined the movement in 2011. From the experiences she has had since then, she has gotten to know what she is truly capable of. She was hired as a secretary and is, among other duties, responsible for registering all families. She speaks brightly and very calmly about how much she likes to know the stories of these families, how much she grew up and better understands the world and herself as a whole.

Priscila Neves: “E hoje eu penso que o que eu quero fazer eu vou fazer. Antigamente meu mundinho era fechado. Já tinha meu filho quando entrei no movimento. Hoje em dia meu filho participa das lutas comigo e sabe da importância dessa luta. Levo ele comigo sempre que posso.”

Priscila Neves: Today I believe that I am capable of doing all that I’ve dreamed. In the old days my little world was closed. I was already a mother when I joined the movement. Nowadays my son participates in the struggle with me and knows the importance of it. I take him with me to all events I can.

1 The immense amount of collected material will result in at least two feature documentaries: the first is almost finished and the second is looking for financial support so it can be edited.

Housing the Co-op

Glossary

A **Adequate housing:** Adequate housing was recognized as part of the right to an adequate standard of living in international instruments including the 1948 Universal Declaration of Human Rights and in the 1966 International Covenant on Economic, Social and Cultural Rights. A number of conditions must be met before particular forms of shelter can be considered to constitute adequate housing. Housing is not adequate if its cost threatens or compromises the occupants' enjoyment of other human rights.

B **Bonding and bridging:** The difference between bonding and bridging social capital relates to the nature of the relationships or associations in the social group or community. Bonding social capital is within a group or community whereas bridging social capital is between social groups, social classes, races, religions, or other important socio-demographic or socioeconomic characteristics. The bonding/bridging distinction can be made in relation to a range of relationship and network characteristics. Bridging and bonding social capital can be described as attributes of weak ties and strong ties. Strong ties are related to bonding social capital in that they provide emotional and social support, whereas weak ties (such as acquaintances and colleagues) are associated with bridging social capital. Typically, weak ties are connections between people from different backgrounds and between social networks who provide access to novel information, whereas strong ties serve for the consolidation of relationships.

C **Capacity building:** Capacity building aims at building knowledge, skills, commitment, structures, systems, and leadership models to enable effective self-development. The term is used among intergovernmental organizations to define a country's human, scientific, technological, organizational, institutional, and resource capabilities. A fundamental goal of capacity building is to enhance the ability to evaluate and address the crucial questions related to policy choices and modes of implementation among development options based on an understanding of environment potentials and limits and of needs perceived by the people of the country concerned. According to the United Nations Development Program, capacity building includes the development of human resources as well as of organizational, institutional, and legal frameworks. In regard to human resources, it focuses on the process of equipping individuals with the understanding, skills, and access to information, knowledge, and training that enables them to perform effectively autonomously.

Commoning: Communities are formed and sustained through the sharing of resources and through participation in the governance of the commons, governance that often also envolves direct social labor. Commoning is the active practice for organizing, maintaining, and distributing common goods.

Co-operative housing law: A law that recognizes the co-operative form of ownership with people owning shares in the property as a whole as opposed to a condominium where they own individual units and proportionate shares of the common areas.

Co-operative principles: The seven co-operative principles as promoted by the International Co-operative Alliance (ICA) are:

1 Voluntary and open membership: Co-operatives are voluntary organizations, open to all persons able to use their services and willing to accept the responsibilities of membership, without gender, social, racial, political or religious discrimination.

2 Democratic member control: Co-operatives are democratic organizations controlled by their members, who actively participate in setting their policies and making decisions. Men and women serving as elected representatives are accountable to the members. In primary co-operatives members have equal voting rights (one member, one vote) and co-operatives at other levels are also organized in a democratic manner.

3 Member economic participation: Members contribute equitably to, and democratically control, the capital of their co-operative. At least part of that capital is usually the common property of the co-operative. Members usually receive limited compensation, if any, on capital subscribed as a condition of membership. Members allocate surpluses for any or all of the following purposes: developing theirco-operative, possibly by setting up reserves, part of which at least would be indivisible; benefiting members in proportion to their transactions with the co-operative; and supporting other activities approved by the membership.

4 Autonomy and independence: Co-operatives are autonomous, self-help organizations controlled by their members. If they enter into agreements with other organizations, including governments, or raise capital from external sources, they do so on terms that ensure democratic control by their members and maintain their co-operative autonomy.

5 Education, training, and information: Co-operatives provide education and training for their members, elected representatives, managers, and employees so they can contribute effectively to the development of their co-operatives. They inform the general public – particularly young people and opinion leaders – about the nature and benefits of cooperation.

6 Cooperation among co-operatives: Co-operatives serve their members most effectively and strengthen the co-operative movement by working together through local, national, regional, and international structures.

7 Concern for community: Co-operatives work for the sustainable development of their communities through policies approved by their members.

Co-production: Coined by Elinor Ostrom and her colleagues in the late 1970s, co-production refers to a service delivery model that equally involves the public sector and private citizens. Co-production reframes the way traditional public services are recognized: people are no longer only passive consumers and beneficiaries of public products but are active agents who conceive, design, and manage services together with the public authorities. Expanding the notion of participatory practices, co-production is not just a phase of a consultation process but is truly embedded in everyday lives by engaging communities and authorities to provide, steer, and deliver services in a mutual, long-term relationship.

E **Empowerment:** Empowerment describes a process that allows people to take greater control over the decisions, assets, policies, processes, and institutions that affect their lives. This means to enable certain groups—in particular women—to act in the social, economic, political, and legal domains by granting or reenforcing rights, abilities, as well as access to facilities that were previously denied to them.

G **Gated communities:** Gated communities are residential communities that are exclusionary or segregated and have a physical barrier or guards to keep non-residents out. A subdivision or neighborhood, often surrounded by a barrier, to which entry is restricted to residents and their guests. This might be for reasons of security, or fear, or it might be for social status as well as for the higher real estate prices that an appearance of exclusivity and the like may bring.

H **Habitability:** Housing is not adequate if it does not guarantee physical safety or provide adequate space as well as protection against the cold, damp, heat, rain, wind, other threats to health, and structural hazards.

I **Inclusivity:** Inclusivity in planning recognizes that every person has the right to participate in shaping the built environment and to benefit from urban development. It places particular focus on the most marginalized and vulnerable groups of society by promoting participation in planning processes and also diversity in representation. Inclusive cities enable everyone access to services, jobs, and opportunities and to be part of the city's civic and political life.

Informal sector: The informal sector, also known as the underground economy, black economy, shadow economy, or gray economy, is part of a country's economy that is not recognized as a normal income source. People who work in the informal sector do not declare their income and pay no taxes on them. The term includes illegal activities such as drug pushing and smuggling. It also includes cleaning car windshields at traffic lights or doing construction work, i.e., legal work.

The informal sector includes two categories: first, all unregistered commercial enterprises; second, all noncommercial enterprises that have no formal structure in terms of organization and operation. Although the informal sector makes up a significant portion of the economies in developing countries, it is often stigmatized as troublesome and unmanageable. However, the informal sector provides critical economic opportunities for the poor and has been expanding rapidly since the 1960s. Integrating the informal economy into the formal sector is an important policy challenge.

Informal settlements: Informal settlements are residential areas where inhabitants are deemed by the authorities to have no legal claim to the land they occupy and the system of occupation ranges from squatting to informal rental housing. In most cases, the housing is insecure and poor quality and does not comply with current planning and building regulations. Informal settlements are also often situated in the most precarious urban areas where basic services and infrastructure including public or green space are limited.

Informality: Informality is, by definition, a question of the relationship of individuals and communities with the law: informal being in some way not in compliance with recognized law. In many urban areas, significant proportions (often a majority) of the population are affected by informality in their employment, housing, or tenure status. Informal organization is characterized by an absence of legal licenses, titles, and regulatory supervision. Residents in informal housing may have no recognized rights, making eviction an ever-present threat. Informal businesses operate without licenses and do not pay taxes. Informality is frequently the result of inadequate, inappropriate, or ineffective formal policies or legal frameworks that regulate activities based on assumptions regarding the socioeconomic environment that do not reflect realities on the ground. This results in a situation in many cities where the laws, institutions, and policies governing economic, social, and political affairs deny a large part of society the chance to participate on equal terms. Most poor people do not live under the shelter of the law and the opportunities it affords. Because the poor lack recognized rights, they are vulnerable to abuse. A minority of the world's population can take advantage of legal norms and regulations. Despite this vulnerability, it is important to note that informality does not mean that there is no system, merely that what does exist is not formally recognized. Informal local norms and institutions, including those of a traditional or customary nature, govern lives and livelihoods.

Information and communications technology: Information and communications technology (ICT) is an extensional term for information technology (IT) that stresses the role of unified communications and the integration of telecommunications (telephone lines and wireless signals) and computers as well as necessary enterprise software, middleware, storage, and audiovisual systems that enable users to access, store, transmit, and manipulate information.

International Co-operative Alliance: Founded in 1895, the International Co-operative Alliance (ICA) is the largest co-operative federation, representing over 300 co-operative associations and organizations in over 100 countries. Counting all co-operative members of the alliance, the ICA represents almost one billion individuals worldwide.

The ICA promotes and supports all major sectors, including agriculture, banking, insurance, health, consumer and housing co-operatives. In this function, the ICA not only acts as a platform for exchange and networking, but also maintains and develops the core principles and values of the co-operative movement.

L

Land trust: A land trust or community land trust (CLT) is a nonprofit corporation that develops and stewards affordable housing, community gardens, civic buildings, commercial spaces, and other community assets on behalf of a community.

Local economic development (LED): LED is a participatory development process that encourages partnership arrangements with representatives from all sectors (government, private, nongovernment) to provide a road map between the main private and public stakeholders in a defined territory. With a multidisciplinary approach, LED enables the joint design and implementation of common development strategies by making use of local resources as well as competitive advantages. Preventing purely top-down decision-making, the micro-economic approach of LED has the objective to create more resilient, inclusive, and sustainable cities rooted in local economic activities and processes.

M

Microcredit: Microcredit is a small amount of money loaned to a client by a bank or other institution. Microcredit can be offered, often without collateral, to an individual or through group lending. Part of the field of microfinance, microcredit is the provision of credit services to low-income entrepreneurs.

Micro-politics: The importance of micro-politics as a type of political regulation involved in shaping the preferences, attitudes, and perceptions of individual subjects was already defined by French philosophers Michel Foucault, Gilles Deleuze, and Félix Guattari in the second half of the twentieth century. While macro-politics is based on legal power and the institutional regulation of behavior, micro-political techniques depend on instilling the attitudes, dispositions, skills, and capacities to shape behavior. Micro-politics contributes to the formation of desire, belief, inclination, and judgment in political processes and therefore has a more substantial impact on the production of subjectivity.

The question of how micro-politics contributes to political change and the formation of revolutionary movements was addressed by Suely

Rolnik and Félix Guattari in their joint research and publication on the situation of Brazil after the end of the military regime. Extending the influence of micro-political forces on the formation of desires and beliefs, Guattari and Rolnik refer to micro-politics as the "politics of unconsciousness," and they describe how the "colonial unconscious" corresponds to the mode of desire production in worldwide integrated capitalism, which today predominates everywhere and drives all spheres of human life.

Multilevel governance: This is a decision-making system to define and implement public policies produced by a collaborative relation vertically (between different levels of government) or horizontally (within the same level, e.g., between ministries or between local governments) or both. It also includes the partnership with actors from civil society and the private sector for the achievement of common goals. In order to be effective, multilevel governance should be rooted in the principle of subsidiarity, the respect for local autonomy, and establish mechanisms of trust and structured dialogue.

Mutirão (mutual self-help): The term *mutirão* originates from the indigenous Tupi language and stands for "joint effort," meaning the practice of mutual self-help work in order to obtain a result not possible to be achieved by one person only. Derived from the indigenous cultural understanding of a close community that rejects solely individual endeavors for the greater prosperity of the community, the concept was appropriated during the 1980s for the Brazilian movements of self-help schemes based on collaboration, solidarity, and cooperation to achieve common social, political, and development goals. The appropriated concept stands for collective mobilizations described originally for work in the field or the construction of social housing, in which all are beneficiaries while at the same time helping, in a system of rotation without hierarchy. Currently, by extension of meaning, mutirão can designate any collective initiative for the execution of an unpaid service as a joint effort.

N

Neighborhood upgrading: A program providing services to informal settlements, neighborhood upgrading usually consists of a menu of services that are provided to the beneficiaries, including but not limited to access to infrastructure such as water supply, sanitation systems, electricity, garbage cleanup, and social services such as schools, daycare, and health clinics.

New Urban Agenda: Developed during the Habitat III conference in 2016, the New Urban Agenda is a document instructing the development, function, and sustainable design of cities. The agenda makes clear demands: compact settlement development with adequate space, a sparing use of resources, a strenghtening of public transport, and healthy living conditions for all in cities. It therefore becomes a toolbox for actors at the local level. It functions as a guideline and political reinforcement in the commitment to sustainable and integrated urban development. The New Urban Agenda is also an essential building block for the implementation of the UN Sustainable Development Goals (SDGs), in particular SDG 11, "Make cities and human settlements inclusive, safe, resilient and sustainable," as well as for decisions about energy-saving and renewable-energy-promoting urban development stated at the UN Climate Change Conference COP 21 in Paris. Although the New Urban Agenda is a nonbinding agreement, it is of great value to municipalities, for it offers clear instructions and guidelines for the implementation of sustainable urban development.

P

Participatory slum upgrading: This is a methodological approach that aims to improve urban development power imbalances. It puts all stakeholders, especially slum dwellers, at the heart of the process to improve slums' living conditions. This multi-stakeholder platform is considered more likely to promote the necessary partnerships, governance arrangements, institutional structures, and financing options that result in inclusive planning and sustainable outcomes.

Political ecology: Political ecology is the study of the relationships between political, economic, and social factors with environmental issues and changes. Political ecology differs from apolitical ecological studies by politicizing environmental issues and phenomena. The academic discipline offers wide-ranging studies integrating ecological social sciences with political economy in topics such as degradation and marginalization, environmental conflict, conservation and control, and environmental identities and social movements.

Principles of managing the commons: Opposed to Garrett Hardin's widely disseminated text "The Tragedy of the Commons," in *Governing the Commons* Elinor Ostrom paints a different picture of how the commons can be maintained in the long run. Based on extensive fieldwork, she establishes that a commons is not just a free resource open to everybody to exploit but is a highly complex setup of self-organized management of a natural resource. Through her study of long-lasting, successful commons worldwide, Ostrom identifies a set of eight principles that ultimately allow a sustainable management of the commons: 1. Define clear group boundaries; 2. Match rules governing use of common goods to local needs and conditions; 3. Ensure that those affected by the rules can participate in modifying the rules; 4. Make sure the rule-making rights of community members are respected by outside authorities; 5. Develop a system, carried out by community members, for monitoring members' behavior; 6. Use graduated sanctions for rule violators; 7. Provide accessible, low-cost means for dispute resolution; 8. Build responsibility for governing the common resource in nested tiers, from the lowest level up to the entire interconnected system.

Production of subjectivity: The politics of the production of subjectivity is a question of the relation between a subject and the conditions of its production. It is through the production of subjectivity that we determine and transform the very relations that produce us. For Félix Guattari, the production of subjectivity in contemporary capitalism is organized by mass industries on a global level. It is the first and most important of capitalist productions, because it preconditions and is part of production in all other forms of merchandise. Capitalism organizes the production and control of subjectivity through two different systems that weave together the manufacture of the individuated subject (social subjection) and what seems to be the opposite, de-subjectification (machinic enslavement). Therefore capitalism exercises a twofold hold over subjectivity.

R

Right to adequate housing: Article 25 (1) of the Universal Declaration of Human Rights states, "Everyone has the right to a standard of living adequate for the health and well-being of himself and of his family, including food, clothing, housing and medical care and necessary social services, and the right to security in the event of unemployment, sickness, disability, widowhood, old age or other lack of livelihood in circumstances beyond his control." Additionally, Article 11 (1) of the International Covenant on Economic, Social, and Cultural Rights states, "The States Parties to the present Covenant recognize the right of everyone to an adequate standard of living for himself and his family, including adequate food, clothing and housing, and to the continuous improvement of living conditions." This is further articulated in the Committee on Economic, Social and Cultural Rights, general comment No. 4 (1991) on the right to adequate housing. According to the United Nations Fact Sheet 21, the right to adequate housing contains freedoms and entitlements. The freedoms include: protection against forced evictions, arbitrary destruction, and demolition of one's home; the right to be free from arbitrary interference with one's home, privacy, and family; and the right to choose one's residence, to determine where to live and freedom of movement. The entitlements include: security of tenure; housing, land, and property restitution; equal and nondiscriminatory access to adequate housing; and participation in housing-related decision-making at the national and community levels.

Right to the city: The World Charter for the Right to the City defines the right to the city as the equitable usufruct of cities within the principles of sustainability, democracy, equity, and social justice. It is the collective right of the inhabitants of cities, in particular of the vulnerable and marginalized groups, that confers upon them legitimacy of action and organization based on their uses and customs, with the objective to achieve full exercise of the right to free self-determination and an adequate standard of living. The Right to the City is interdependent with all internationally recognized and integrally conceived human rights, and therefore includes all the civil, political, economic, social, cultural, and environmental rights that are already regulated in the international human-rights treaties.

S **Self-government:** Self-government describes the capacity of local governments to manage public affairs in the interests of the local population and within the limits of the law as recognized by national legislation. These rights and responsibilities may be political (capacity to elect their own government bodies, make policies, take decisions, and exercise their function independently from other government spheres on matters related to their competencies), financial (capacity to access adequate resources to carry out their responsibilities and use them freely), or administrative (capacity for self-organization).

Social capital: Social capital broadly refers to those factors of effectively functioning social groups that include such things as interpersonal relationships, a shared sense of identity, a shared understanding, shared norms, shared values, trust, cooperation, and reciprocity. The term generally refers to (a) resources and the value of these resources, both tangible (public spaces, private property) and intangible ("actors," "human capital," people), (b) the relationships among these resources, and (c) the impact that these relationships have on the resources involved in each relationship and on larger groups. It is generally seen as a form of capital that produces public goods for a common good. Social capital has been used to explain the improved performance of diverse groups, the growth of entrepreneurial firms, superior managerial performance, enhanced supply-chain relations, the value derived from strategic alliances, and the evolution of communities.

Social function of the city: The social function of the city is one of the main pillars of sustainable cities, the other two pillars being the economic and the environmental structure of urban districts. This balanced triangle guarantees quality of urban life. The social function of the city is concerned with inclusive livability and social cohesion in urban territories. The development of methods, design tools, and policies to implement socially sustainable solutions in collaboration with citizens, politicians, and corporations is the main challenge of socially inclusive cities. A common definition of social urban goals is needed and varies in terms of parameters (demographic structure, number of pedestrians, cyclists, restaurants, shopping facilities, central heating, education, jobs, sanitation, safety, access to housing, rent stability, diversity, etc.). The Social Cities Index is a method to measure the social sustainability in cities. The index identifies the parameters and indicators that have the greatest effect on social function and sustainability in cities.

Social housing: Social housing commonly refers to a national housing system that is provided using public subsidies directed to lowering rents which is allocated via nonmarket mechanisms. The core components of a social housing system include: development promotion regime (having a privileged, competitive, or subordinate position in the land market); rent setting regime (approaches include cost rent, nominal rent, and market rent); an eligibility and allocation regime (whether universal, segmented, or targeted/restricted); an operating cost and profit regime (nonprofit, limited profit, and for profit); and the market position of different providers (private, third sector, and public).

Solidarity economy: Social and solidarity economy refers to enterprises and organizations (co-operatives, mutual benefit societies, associations, foundations, and social enterprises) which produce goods, services, and knowledge that meet the needs of the community they serve through the pursuit of specific social and environmental objectives and the fostering of solidarity.

Sustainable Development Goals: The Sustainable Development Goals (SDGs) are a collection of seventeen global goals set by the United Nations General Assembly in 2015 to be achieved by the year 2030.
These are: (1) no poverty, (2) zero hunger, (3) good health and well-being, (4) quality education, (5) gender equality, (6) clean water and sanitation, (7) affordable and clean energy, (8) decent work and economic growth, (9) industry, innovation, and infrastructure, (10) reducing inequality, (11) sustainable cities and human settlements, (12) responsible consumption and production, (13) climate action, (14) life below water, (15) life on land, (16) peace, justice, and strong institutions, (17) partnerships for the goals. The goals are accompanied by 169 targets and indicators to measure the progress made and to offer transparency and greater understanding of each goal. The co-operative practice is unique, for it enables a sustainable, practical, and democratic way to tackle the challenge of most goals. Specially in regard to SDG 11, "Make cities and human settlements inclusive, safe, resilient and sustainable," the principles of housing co-operatives correspond equally with the goal of a viable model for fast implementation.

Sustainable urbanization: This is the spatial manifestation of urban development processes that create a built environment with norms, institutions, and governance systems enabling individuals, households, and societies to maximize their potential, optimize a vast range of services so that homes and dynamic neighborhoods, cities, and towns are planned, built, renewed, and consolidated, restraining adverse impacts on the environment while safeguarding the quality of life, needs, and livelihood of its present and future populations. As cities moved to the forefront of global socioeconomic change, it came to be accepted that cities not only pose potential threats to sustainable development but also hold promising opportunities for social and economic advancement and for environmental improvements at local, national, and global levels.

U **Urban commons:** Commons were traditionally defined as the elements of the environment (forests, atmosphere, rivers, fisheries, or grazing land) that were shared, used, and enjoyed by all. Today, the commons can also include public goods such as public space, public education, health, and the infrastructure that allows our society to function.

Urban ecology: Urban ecology is the systems-based understanding of biotic and physical elements that occur in urban areas. It recognizes the interaction between natural systems and social and cultural systems, among others. Urban ecology places particular importance on the primacy of natural systems in contributing to livelihoods, well-being, and resilience, and focuses on the interdependence of key resources (usually water, waste, and energy) and their impact on city development. In the policy paper *Urban Ecology and Resilience* (Unit 8) prepared for the United Nations' Habitat III Conference, the term sustainable urban development refers to the normative outcome of policies and actions related to the urban ecology, where "sustainable" is defined as the state wherein natural systems function, remain diverse, and enable the ecosystem to remain in balance.

Urban governance: Urban governance is the software that enables the urban hardware to function, the enabling environment requiring the adequate legal frameworks, efficient political, managerial, and administrative processes, as well as strong and capable local institutions able to respond to the citizens' needs.

Colophon

Editing: Sascha Delz, Rainer Hehl, Patricia Ventura
Art direction and graphic design: Something Fantastic Art Department with Rainer Hehl and Fernanda Tellez Velasco
Copyediting: Max Bach, Esmé Rocks
Printing: Printon
Typeface: Helvetica Neue, Times
Paper: Holmen 70 g

This publication was made possible with the significant support of various people and institutions. The editors would like to thank Prof. Dr. Marc Angélil at the Department of Architecture (D-Arch) of ETH Zurich for his generous intellectual and financial support throughout the project. The underlying research was funded by a substantial grant from the Swiss National Science Foundation (SNF) and greatly benefited from a research partnership formed with Luciana Corrêa do Lago and Ricardo Gouvêa Corrêa from the Instituto de Pesquisa e Planejamento Urbano e Regional (IPPUR) of the Universidade Federal Rio de Janeiro (UFRJ). Finally, the editors would like to express their gratitude to all the contributing authors for their unhesitant collaboration and for sharing their work and expertise.

Die Deutsche Bibliothek lists this publication in the Deutsche Nationalbibliographie; detailed bibliographic data is available on the internet at http://dnb.de.

Ruby Press
Schönholzer Str. 11
10115 Berlin
Germany

www.ruby-press.com
book@ruby-press.com

Printed in Estonia
ISBN 978-3-944074-47-4